THE SCARECROW

THE SCARECROW

Fact and Fable

Peter Haining

ROBERT HALE · LONDON

© *Peter Haining 1988*
First published in Great Britain 1988

British Library Cataloguing in Publication Data

Haining, Peter
 The scarecrow : fact and fable
 1. Scarecrows
 I. Title
 632

ISBN 0-7090-3316-8

Robert Hale Limited
Clerkenwell House
Clerkenwell Green
London EC1R 0HT

Set in Sabon by Derek Doyle & Associates, Mold, Clwyd
Printed in Great Britain by
St Edmundsbury Press Ltd, Bury St Edmunds, Suffolk
and bound by WBC Bookbinders Limited

Contents

List of Illustrations   7
Acknowledgements   11

1   The World of the Scarecrow   13
2   A History of the Mawkin   28
3   The Scarecrow in Literature   63
4   The Straw Man on the Screen   103
5   The Twentieth-Century Scarecrow   145

Appendix: How to Make a Scarecrow   173

Bibliography   179
Index   183

Illustrations

'The World's Favourite Scarecrow'	12
Bisexual garden scarecrow in Norfolk	14
Television's favourite scarecrow	16
The Marquis of Bath's son dressed as a scarecrow	18
Labour Party MP Michael Foot as Worzel Gummidge	20
One of many cartoon scarecrow images	22
Rupert Bear from the *Daily Express*	23
Fred Basset of the *Daily Mail* meets a scarecrow	24
World War II cartoon by E.H. Shepard	25
'Old Jem' on duty at Lord's Cricket Ground	27
Title page of the first work to mention scarecrows	29
An illustration from *The Art of Rhetorique*	30
A recent edition of William Cobbett's classic work, *Rural Rides*	33
The young Cobbett caricatured by James Gillray	36
'The Farmer's Friend' by George Cruickshank	39
The bold-looking mawkin of Old Castle Farm	43
Nineteenth-century sketch of a young bird-scarer	46
Bird-scarer from the film *Captain Clegg*	49
Punch comment on the job of bird-scaring	52
Modern bird-scarers in Kent	54
The ancient tradition of protecting crops	56
Corn figures in a straw dance	59
The effect of the 'ugly figure'	61
The most famous scarecrow in literature	64
William Shakespeare – the man who immortalized the scarecrow	66
Robinson Crusoe	69
The Devil brings the scarecrow, Feathertop, to life	73
A ragged character from the *Westminster Review*	76
Frank Baum's scarecrow, sketched by W.W. Denslow	79

Roy Krenkel's scarecrow	81
Sketch from Edith King Hall's *The Story of the Scarecrow*	84
Russell Thorndike, the creator of the famous Doctor Syn	90
The original concept of Worzel Gummidge as drawn by Elizabeth Alldridge	92
Broadcaster David Kossoff's sketch of Worzel Gummidge	95
Gummidge as portrayed in Southern Television's production	96
Illustration by Irene Hawkins for Walter de la Mare's *The Scarecrow*	98
Cover illustration from *The Countryman*	101
Patrick McGoohan in the title role of *Doctor Syn, Alias The Scarecrow*	104
Cecil Hepworth: creator of the short comedy *The Scarecrow*	105
Fred Stone who, with his partner, David Montgomery, first brought to life Frank Baum's scarecrow	107
William Selig's 'Fairylogue' led to the movie *His Majesty, The Scarecrow of Oz* made in 1914	109
Hollywood comedian Larry Semon	112
Buster Keaton playing a man of straw	115
The man of straw becomes a human being in *Puritan Passions*	116
The mysterious scarecrow look-out in *Captain Clegg*	118
Russell Thorndike's hero in *Doctor Syn Alias The Scarecrow*	120
Ray Bolger in the 1939 MGM film, *The Wizard of Oz*	121
Bolger filming with Judy Garland	125
Michael Jackson in *The Wiz*	127
The Walt Disney film, *Return to Oz*	130
Cartoon version of the scarecrow in *Journey Back To Oz*	132
Don Blackwell as the farmer persecuted into madness by scarecrows	134
John Carradine, looking for all the world like a ragged scarecrow	136
Television's first Worzel Gummidge, Frank Atkinson	139
Behind-the-scenes transformation of Jon Pertwee	141
Promotions which have featured Worzel Gummidge	143

LIST OF ILLUSTRATIONS

A.L. Collins' portrait of a scarecrow armed with a blunderbuss	147
Humorous drawings by Terry Willers of Irish scarecrows	148
A Scottish Tattie-Bogle on duty in Perthshire	153
A fearsome French tableau of scarecrows	155
Russian satirical cartoon from *Krokodil* magazine	157
Japanese cartoon of a farmer frightened by his own scarecrow!	159
Chilling front cover of *Fear!* magazine	160
Scarecrows equipped with video cameras	162
Field Smith's comment on the idea of female scarecrows	163
The Lady Diana scarecrow which started a new fashion in July 1981!	165
Devonshire farmer Bruce Burton's statuesque Venus de Milo bird-scarer	167
A bevy of beautiful scarecrows	169
Scarecrows that SCARE	171
Do-it-yourself scarecrow from *Punch*	174
Choosing scarecrow names!	176
A unique scarecrow by the ingenious W. Heath Robinson	177
The distinctive symbol of Scarecrow Press Inc.	179
The author's daughter, Gemma, with the family scarecrows	180

The author is grateful to the following for supplying the photographs and illustrations appearing in this book: Pip Miller, David Collins, W.W. Denslow, Roy Krenkel, Martin Honeysett, Elizabeth Alldridge, Jill Crockford, David Kossoff, Irene Hawkins, A.L. Collins, Terry Willers, Stan Fine, Keith Waite, Laurence Pollinger Ltd., Southern Television, BBC Enterprises, Associated Newspapers, Times Newspapers Ltd., Express Newspapers, Observer Newspapers, *Punch*, the *Countryman*, Faber & Faber, Columbia Pictures, MGM Pictures, Hammer Films, Walt Disney Pictures and United Artists.

For
Pip Miller
A scarecrow enthusiast too!

Acknowledgements

The author would like to thank the following people and companies for their help in the writing of this book and also for permission to use copyright material: Pip Miller, W.O.G. Lofts, Jon Pertwee, Dr Jacqueline Simpson, A.G. Street, Fred Kitchen, Henry Williamson, B.A. Wherry, Ray Palmer, Bob Copper, E.C. Palmer, Henry P. Maskell, Gwendolyn Wormser, Vera Menteth, Sir Hugh Walpole, Alfred Noyes, Clemence Dane, Russell Thorndike, Barbara Euphan Todd, Walter de la Mare, James Thurber, Ray Bolger, Cormac MacConnell, W.D. Crocker, Willie Soutar, Michael Williams, Suzy Gale, Elizabeth Seager and Barbara Hargreaves. Thanks also to these newspapers: *The Times*, *Observer*, *Sunday Times*, *Sunday Express*, *Private Eye*, *Daily Telegraph*, *Daily Express*, *Country Life*, *Punch*, *Daily Mail*, *Folklore*, *The Treasury*, *London Standard*, *Cara*, *Hollywood Reporter*, *Time Magazine*, *Morning Star*, the *Scotsman*, *Campbeltown Courier*, *Scots Magazine*, *New York Times*, *Guardian*, *Sunday People*, *Mail on Sunday*, *Sunday Mirror*, *Sunday Telegraph*, and *Amateur Gardening*. Grateful thanks are also extended to these publishers for allowing quotations from their publications: Batsford Books, Grafton Books, Macmillan, The Bodley Head, Blackie Children's Books, Penguin, Cassell Ltd., E.P. Dutton & Co and Faber & Faber. Photographs and stills have also been provided by BBC TV, Southern TV, British Film Institute, Hammer Films, Walt Disney Organisation, MGM Films and Columbia Pictures. While the author has taken every care over the use of copyright material in this book, in the case of any accidental infringement please write to him care of his publishers.

'The World's Favourite Scarecrow' – Ray Bolger in *The Wizard of OZ* (1939)

1   The World of the Scarecrow

'Scarecrow: an image or clapper set up to frighten birds.'

SAMUEL JOHNSON

In early February 1986 the letters page of *The Times* was suddenly enlivened by an unexpected exchange of correspondence on the subject of scarecrows. Where, in previous weeks, writers to the newspaper had argued about matters of state and world affairs in general, the page was now absorbed by a debate as to whether the scarecrow still existed in the countryside – and, more particularly, whether the figure had any use in modern agriculture or should be considered a relic of the past deserving no more than a footnote in rural history. The writers were vociferous in their views, and no doubt readers of that distinguished paper were more than a little surprised at the weight of interest that was shown. This interest itself was to prove a significant pointer to answering the question which the correspondence posed.

The debate was set in motion by a West Yorkshire doctor, Paul Fursdon of Huddersfield, who enquired innocently enough on 12 February: 'The farming landscapes seen from the carriage windows are as lovely as ever. But the one thing I miss above all else is the scarecrow. There do not seem to be any left. Has no one time for this endangered species of art form? Seeing them in my boyhood added to the pleasures of the journey. Perhaps British Rail could offer prizes?'

It has to be said that letters of this kind are by no means unusual in the pages of *The Times*. Any diligent researcher going through back issues of the paper will have no difficulty in finding many similar off-beat subjects which have been raised over the years. Many, though, have garnered nothing other than a resounding silence from the newspaper's readers. Not so scarecrows. According to *The Times*' letters editor, the response was one of the biggest for such a subject in recent years. In fact, he was able to use only a very small percentage of the mail which reached his desk. As ever, though, the selection he made was both interesting and revealing.

A Berkshire reader, James Pickard, from Hare Hatch near Twyford, was the first to have his response in print. 'Dr Fursdon is right to cherish nostalgic feelings about the absence of the lonely and hardworking scarecrow,' he wrote. 'I suspect that it is also sorely missed by some members of the animal kingdom as well: the one recently erected in a field adjacent to my house is at the moment providing invaluable shelter from the east wind for a family of shivering pheasants.'

If Mr Pickard's letter indicated that scarecrows were still being made, the fact was quickly underlined by other writers. Mrs Catherine Larthe of Brimpsfield Park in Gloucester was

One of many scarecrows photographed by Pip Miller. A curiously bisexual garden scarecrow in Norfolk dressed in a skirt with a football head!

one of these. 'Let Dr Paul Fursdon take heart,' she wrote. 'Scarecrows may be endangered, but they are not yet extinct, they just keep away from railway lines and need to be visited on foot.' And showing herself to be not only a scarecrow admirer but also a maker of them, Mrs Larthe added, 'Ours wears the family's cast-off (or commandeered) clothing and looks so like the ex-owners that the dogs will keep rushing across the fields to them expecting walks!'

Another admirer, the Hon. Mrs Iris Cawley of Hindhead, Surrey, also had a story to tell about the efficiency of a scarecrow.

'A couple of years ago,' she wrote on 17 February, 'when we ran a strawberry farm in Worcestershire, I glanced up and noticed a man and a woman obviously getting ready to pick my neighbour's lovely black cherries. As I was hoping to buy a lot to bottle I nipped over the fence to have a word with them, only to find, when I was only about 20 yards away, that they were beautiful dummies suspended from the branches and moving very slightly in the breeze! Incidentally, they fooled the birds, too – it was a bountiful crop.'

Mrs Cawley also reinforced Catherine Larthe's statement that the ' ... art form is by no means dead', although she doubted whether ' ... today's examples will be seen from the attenuated rail system'.

The most compelling piece of evidence of the scarecrow's continued existence came from an unexpected but none the less convincing source: Robin W. Batchelor of the Hot-Air Balloon Company in London, who could literally claim a bird's-eye view on the whole issue.

'I agree with Dr Fursdon when he expressed his desire to see more scarecrows from his railway carriage window,' he wrote on 22 February, 'so I suggest he tries another means of transport which will leisurely carry him across areas rarely seen by others: a balloon.

'Having been a professional balloonist for 15 years, my work has taken me to nearly all parts of the British Isles and I can assure Dr Fursdon that the scarecrow is still to be found. In fact, one example was so good I called down to ask where I was!'

Jonathan Bates from Edinburgh reported that scarecrows

were also very much in evidence north of the border – but nowadays, he said, they had '... developed in much the same way that art is supposed to have developed'. Writing on 24 February, he commented, 'Many of today's scarecrows consist of a pole surmounted by a bin liner or similar plastic sheet – a punk scarecrow, perhaps – whilst others are vaguely mechanical in appearance. I have even spotted cubist scarecrows

Television's favourite scarecrow, Worzel Gummidge as played by Jon Pertwee, with just a few of his many young fans

during recent walks in the countryside. However, like Dr Fursdon, I much prefer the traditional variety.'

This letter shared *The Times*' columns with another from an actual manufacturer of one of these new breed of scarecrows, Ray Jackson of King's Lynn in Norfolk, who wrote: 'We have just obtained the marketing rights in the UK for a novel birdscaring device – a tough, PVC inflatable "man" mounted on a pole to pivot and move. When dressed in old clothes this new scarecrow – called "Jon Doe" – does in fact look exceptionally realistic and is much less of a task to erect than the good old-fashioned "Worzel Gummidge" type.'

Despite Mr Jackson's comments, further evidence of the continued existence of a great many of the 'good-old-fashioned' type of scarecrows was proffered by readers of *The Times* from all over Britain. It neatly underlined my own research into the subject which by then had been going on for some years. Indeed, the evidence I had collected showed that the scarecrow was not merely 'alive' and flourishing in the fields of Britain but still to be found on duty in a great many other parts of the world, too, maintaining its vigil against marauding birds of all kinds. Further, it was to be found featured extensively not only in literature and in films but also in advertising and cartoons, on greetings cards and as a popular media symbol.

All this evidence – and much more – is what the reader will find presented in the pages which follow. Curiously, it is the first survey to have been written about what is, after all, a familiar figure of the countryside.

The Times is not, however, the first national newspaper to have focused attention on the scarecrow in recent years. The *Observer*, for example, offers a weekly prize of £25 for the best reader's photograph and has awarded this prize for a scarecrow photograph more times than for any other single subject. The *News of the World's Sunday Magazine* has also shown a liking for similar pictures, predictably those of female scarecrows dressed in revealing clothing.

Perhaps, though, one of the most spectacular demonstrations of public interest followed the *Sunday Express Magazine*'s announcement in May 1981 of a competition to find 'Britain's Cheeriest Scarecrows', with the offer of a first

The Marquis of Bath's son dressed as a scarecrow promoting Longleat House in 1984!

prize of £100. Between then and the closing date at the end of October, over 500 entries were received by the magazine, and actor Jon Pertwee, television's current Worzel Gummidge, selected the winning entry.

Reporting on the photographs, the *Sunday Express* said: 'Entries included such oddities as a bride scarecrow, a dinosaur scarecrow, and a scarecrow in the stocks. Several readers photographed the same scarecrows. Some of the specimens looked so realistic that Worzel Gummidge insisted they must be people dressed up. Actually they were shop dummies!'

The magazine continued, 'Gummidge is highly suspicious of new fangled scarecrows like these. He is especially worried about electronic scaring devices. He says they'll be doing traditional scarecrows like himself out of a job, and then where will he go?'

Jon Pertwee admitted that he had been 'astonished' at the number of entries, and what with 10,000 and more people turning out to meet him when he made personal appearances around the country, 'I just didn't realise that scarecrows had so many friends.'

Jon Pertwee is himself an example of the extraordinary power of the scarecrow on popular imagination. The measure of his achievement was commented upon by *The Times*' television critic in March 1982: 'Until you have seen Jon Pertwee's scarecrow, you do not know what brilliance of production and acting it calls for to infuse life into bits of rag and bundles of straw.'

The image of Worzel Gummidge has cropped up in a number of interesting circumstances. In October 1982, for instance, the Reverend Stuart Foster, vicar of St Mark's Church, Basingstoke, appeared in his pulpit dressed as Gummidge in order to try to attract more people to his services. Though there were some complaints about his 'eccentric appearance', over 400 people packed the pews for 'Worzel's harvest festival', as one report described it. And in June 1984 Christopher Thynne, son of the Marquis of Bath, dressed up as a scarecrow to help promote a visit by Jon Pertwee to the family's ancestral home, Longleat House. His ingenious stunt earned him a report in the *Daily Mail*'s prestigious gossip column by Nigel Dempster, plus a photograph.

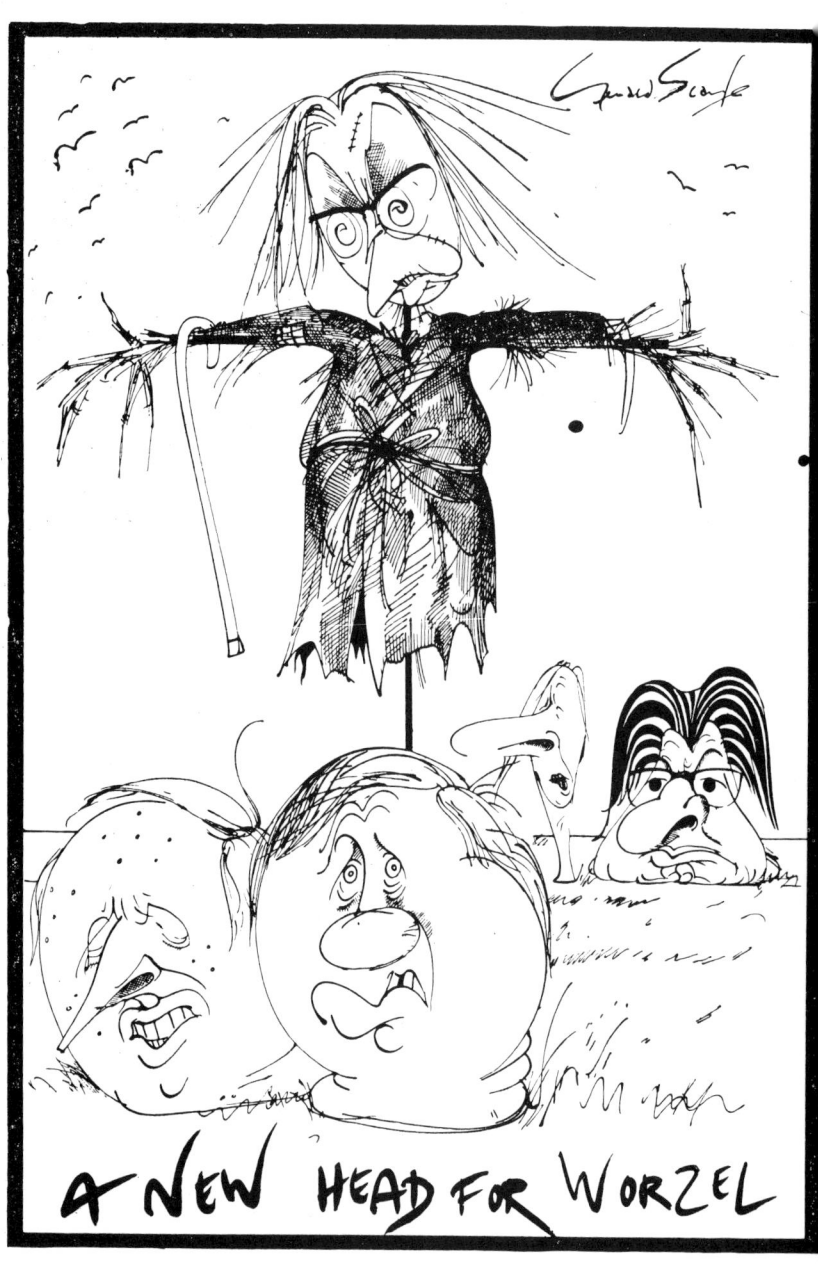

One of the many cartoons of Labour Party MP Michael Foot as Worzel Gummidge – this one from the *Sunday Times*

However, probably the best-known association with the Worzel Gummidge image has been that of MP Michael Foot who, during his years as leader of the Labour Party, was frequently portrayed as a scarecrow. The image became so widespread that hardly a cartoon of Foot during the year 1981 did not show him resembling Worzel – including one by the television puppet-makers Peter Fluck and Roger Law for *Private Eye* in December 1981, and one of Gerald Scarfe's typically acidic portraits for the *Sunday Times* in June 1983 when a successor to the leadership of the party was being sought. (To be fair, the Tory politician Nigel Lawson has also been shown as a scarecrow under attack from crows seeking monetary gains in a *Daily Telegraph* cartoon published in March 1986.)

Dozens of other cartoonists have employed the scarecrow image in topics ranging from straw burning to rural development and the encroachment of the press on the royal family's privacy. Popular newspaper strip-cartoon characters like the *Daily Express*'s Rupert Bear have also encountered scarecrows in their adventures, and again I have picked a typical example to represent a great many more.

In the world of advertising the scarecrow has been used to promote everything from country clothes to the London Docks Authority scheme to encourage new development in its area. 'Why rusticate in the country?' a scarecrow was shown asking in one of the Authority's posters, 'when the heart of London is free for exploitation?' The scarecrow has also promoted beer (Ruddles), chocolates (comedian Neil Innes dressed as a scarecrow who comes to life to 'have a break from scaring crows' by eating a Kit-Kat bar) and cigarettes (an American brand, Newport Lights).

Contests to find the best scarecrow have become popular in recent years, and this idea seems to owe its origin to a Shropshire farmer named Henry Sedge. In the early 1950s he started to dot his fields with the occasional scarecrow either kneeling or crouching in a life-like manner. With their apparent success, he next went in for groups, and one of these, three figures set up to look like boys playing marbles, attracted a lot of local attention – as well as that of the press. A report of what happened next can be found in *Country Life* August 1971:

The scarecrow image has been employed by dozens of cartoonists in a wide variety of topics

Soon the Sedge fields were filled with scarecrows of every conceivable kind, in groups and ranks and rings. Their fame spread far and wide. Coach companies of all the principal Midlands towns began to run regular sight-seeing tours of the 'Scarecrow Meadows'. In Coronation Year (1953), Mr Sedge attracted hundreds of thousands of trippers to see Drake Playing Bowls and the Soldiers of the Queen, all done in scarecrows.

But meanwhile Mr Sedge had been neglecting the normal duties of the farmer. He had to sell his livestock, and weeds grew. Fences fell into disrepair. And this, as the Chairman of the County Executive put it, was 'hardly in the best traditions of good husbandry'. So Mr Sedge had his land taken from him, and since his first abortive season at Blackpool (where the sand proved to be too loose to support his creations), nothing more has been heard of him.

One of Britain's most famous strip cartoon characters encounters a scarecrow – Rupert Bear from the *Daily Express*

Though this was the end of Henry Sedge's scarecrows, a group of admirers in the village of Colwich organized a 'Best Scarecrow' contest for the 'Sedge Cup' in 1958 which attracted a dozen entries. From this humble beginning, other contests have been arranged, of which the most successful was undoubtedly that run at Bracknell, Berkshire, in November 1982, when over 900 entries were assembled for judging at the South Hill Park Arts Centre. Runner-up in the contest was a scarecrow like Michael Foot, but the first prize went to a most authentic-looking Prime Minister, Margaret Thatcher.

Another contest, for schoolchildren in Suffolk organized by the Museum of East Anglian Life in Bury St Edmunds in August 1987, attracted an entry of 400 items, mostly scarecrows but also including paintings, poems and original bird-scaring devices – again underlining the strength of the scarecrow tradition.

Indeed, all the research which I have carried out for this book has shown what a fascinating history the scarecrow has enjoyed. In war, as well as peace, he has played a part. During World War I, for instance, 'The Scarecrow' was the code-name for an undercover agent and his team tracking down enemy agents broadcasting messages from Britain to Germany.

In the early days of World War II 'Scarecrow Patrols' were little groups of private pilots flying Tiger Moths who patrolled the skies around Britain while the RAF worked feverishly to build up their squadrons. A number of Home

Fred Basset of the *Daily Mail* meets a scarecrow

THE WORLD OF THE SCARECROW

THE MAN OF STRAW

"It seems ages since I scared anybody."

One of *Punch*'s brilliant World War II cartoons by E.H. Shepard from the issue of 15 October 1941

Guard officers actually disguised themselves as scarecrows to keep watch for an invasion from across the Channel, and German SS Panzer Divisions sometimes disguised snipers as scarecrows to infiltrate the Allied lines. Even in those days, the scarecrow was a favourite image with cartoonists – as the example ridiculing Mussolini from *Punch* of 15 October 1941 shows. (By and large, though, the ordinary scarecrows in the fields had a pretty thin time during both wars, for the shortage of spare clothes meant a good many of them had little more than a few rags to wear.)

In peace-time, the award for the most distinguished service must surely go to 'Old Jem', the scarecrow who keeps the birds off the cricket square at Lord's, the home of English cricket. This redoubtable 'nightwatchman' has guarded the crease for years, and in a tribute on 11 October 1980 the *Daily Mail* said he had ' ... probably done more for English cricket than the Boycotts, Gooches and Bothams can ever do'.

The paper added, 'For Jem, ignoring bad light and rain, is playing a captain's innings by keeping the birds away from the hallowed wicket upon which it is hoped the Australians will falter next year. And Jem is set for a long stay at the crease. He will probably bat through the winter and declare in the Spring.

'If he carries his bat he could even be there for the opening games of the summer. A spokesman at Lord's said that Jem had been named after a groundsman. "They both move at the same speed – but both do a good job," he said.'

My research has also established that the scarecrow has been appearing in literature since the days of Shakespeare (Chapter 3). Appropriately, too, he has his own publishing imprint, Scarecrow Press Inc, which is based in America and which adorns the title pages of its books with a most evocative symbol.

In films for both the cinema and television, the scarecrow has been an enduring figure right back to the very earliest silent, black-and-white movies made at the start of this century. (See Chapter 4.)

But most important of all, of course, has been the continued appearance of the scarecrow in the world's fields and pastures. There have been many changes in his

THE WORLD OF THE SCARECROW

'Old Jem' the famous Lord's Cricket Ground scarecrow on duty

appearance, and the years have similarly seen him develop from a very basic figure, his clothes blowing in the wind, into the latest computer-controlled scarer, moving about vigorously, wailing and often armed with a gun. Such sophisticated scarecrows are not always welcomed, though, as we shall see.

At the same time, I have also discovered a continuation of the old practice of human beings playing bird-scarers. This once well-known rural occupation for men and boys can still be found occasionally.

During the making of this history, the scarecrow has had many different names and these, too, require examination and explanation, as does the puzzle as to *how* the scarecrow was first created and has evolved into the familiar figure we all know and recognize.

The answers to these and other questions are not without surprises ...

2 A History of the Mawkin

'A scarecrow set to frighten fools away'

JOHN DRYDEN

According to the *Oxford English Dictionary*, the word 'scarecrow' has three primary definitions. First, it is a 'device for frightening birds from growing crops, usually a figure of a man dressed in old and ragged clothes'. Secondly, it can be 'a person employed in scaring birds', and thirdly, 'a person whose appearance causes ridicule; a lean; gaunt figure; one who resembles a scarecrow in his dress, a "guy" '. The *OED* adds a further helpful note that it can be 'something (not really formidable) that frightens or is intended to frighten; a "bogy".'

In these precise definitions are encapsulated what I believe are all the elements that have contributed to making the scarecrow such a fascinating and familiar figure of the countryside – and not just that of the British Isles but also in much of the rest of the world.

This first section looks at what little recorded history there is about the straw man – the various other names by which he is known ranging from jackalent to mawkin, hodmadod to mummet and shoy-hoy to tattie-bogle – as well as investigating the greatest mystery of all: just *how* the scarecrow originated.

A search through any of the other of the world's leading dictionaries will offer much the same definition of the scarecrow as that provided by the *OED*, although Joseph Wright, author of *The English Dialect Dictionary* (1903), shows himself to be less of a male chauvinist than his fellow lexicographers, for his entry reads: '*A Scarecrow*: an effigy of a man *or woman*, made of old clothes stuffed with straw, put up in fields to scare birds.'

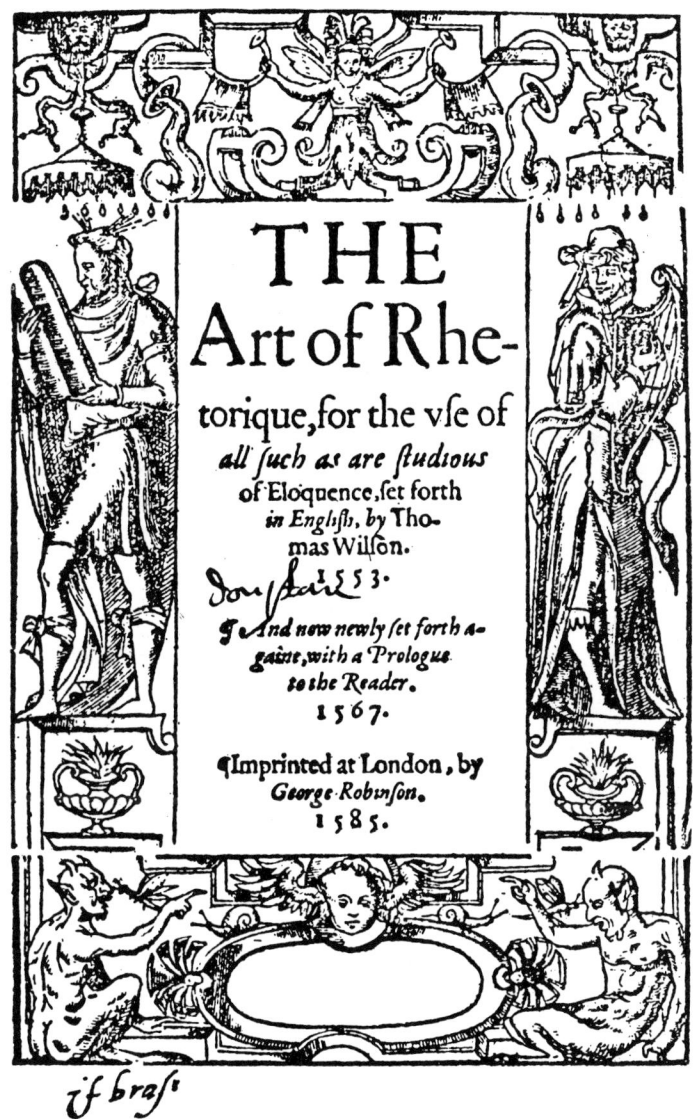

Title page of the first work to mention scarecrows, *The Art of Rhetorique* by Thomas Wilson (1585)

In fact, the scarecrow is such an instantly recognizable figure that few people require an explanation for it, though the younger generation might be a little surprised to learn that people have made their livelihood as scarecrows. What *is* far more surprising is that the scarecrow did not gain an entry into any work of reference until the closing years of the sixteenth century, despite the fact that it had quite evidently been in use by those engaged in growing crops for many generations.

The earliest definition I have been able to locate occurs in an anonymously written work, *Nobody & Somebody*, published in 1791. It contains the following entry which it notes was originally written in the year 1592: 'SCARECROW, A. That which frightens or is intended to frighten without doing physical harm. Literally, that which scares away crows.'

This is *not* the first mention of the scarecrow in print: that occurred some forty years earlier in *The Art of Rhetorique*, a remarkable work of scholarship by Thomas Wilson (1525-81). Wilson was a Lincolnshire man who travelled a

An illustration from a later edition of *The Art of Rhetorique*

great deal in Europe and while visiting the papal Court in Rome became involved in a palace intrigue. He was arrested, charged, tortured and thrown into prison for his 'heretical writings'. In 1559 he daringly escaped and made his way back to England, where tales of his exploits and his facility as a writer made him a favourite at the Court of Queen Elizabeth. Under Her Majesty's patronage he published his book, *The Art of Rhetorique*, which has since been called 'the first English work of criticism'.

Wilson uses several references to his country upbringing while arguing his case for the power of logical reasoning – but perhaps nowhere more vividly than when he is talking about the most effective way to debate important issues, as shown here (with his archaic English translated into a more readable form):

> Not only is it necessary in causes of judgement to consider the scope whereunto we must level our reasons and direct our intentions: but also we ought in every case to have respect unto one special point and chief article: that rather the whole drift of our doings may seem to agree with our first decided purpose. For by this means our judgement shall be framed to speak with discretion, and the ignorant shall learn to perceive with profit whatever is said for his instruction. But they that take upon themselves to talk in open audience, and do not decide beforehand what they will say, shall neither be well liked for their intention, nor allowed for their wit nor esteemed for their learning. For what other thing do they, that bolt out their words in such force, and without all inducement utter out matter, but show themselves to play as young boys or Scare Crows do, which shout in the open and plain fields at all adventurers hitting and missing indiscriminately.

What makes this reference by Thomas Wilson so interesting is that it is not only the first appearance of the word scarecrow in print but also the use of the image of a scarecrow to underline the argument, in which it can be seen as the forerunner of much similar usage that was to follow. Wilson had wittingly or unwittingly come across a symbol that could be powerfully evocative. Equally, the statement demonstrates just how universal the figure of the scarecrow must have been in the minds of Wilson's readers.

Yet, while writers of fiction were to embrace the scarecrow and his image in their works (as shown in Chapter 3), it was to be almost 300 years before the scarecrow was again mentioned in any significant way in a factual context. This next commentator was William Cobbett (1763-1835), author of that classic of country life *Rural Rides*.

Cobbett was born in Farnham, Surrey, the son of a small farmer and the grandson of a day-labourer, so that his whole background was steeped in country ways. Naturally enough, employment on the land seemed inevitable for the boy, and his earliest occupation was acting as a human scarecrow protecting the family crops.

Though the young man did not follow this occupation for long, it was a job that left a lasting impression on him, as he was to observe in an autobiographical sketch written in August 1796: 'I was bred at the plough tail. My first occupation was driving the small birds from the turnip seed, and the rooks from the peas. When I first trudged afield, with my wooden rattle and my satchel swung over my shoulders, I was hardly able to climb the gates and stiles; and, at the close of day, to reach home was a task of infinite difficulty. My next employment was weeding wheat, and leading a single horse at harrowing barley. ... '

Some forty years later, an experienced farmer and also a journalist, Cobbett was working Normanby Farm near Guildford. It was during these years, 1821 to 1826, that he made the journeys which he was to immortalize in *Rural Rides*, published in 1830.

There was little that escaped Cobbett's eye as he rode across the shires, and remembering his early occupation as a 'scarer of small birds', it comes as no surprise to find him mentioning scarecrows in *Rural Rides*, though he refers to them by the dialect name of shoy-hoys, which he explains is an old southern England word imitative of the cry used for scaring off birds from seed corn – the cry he himself had used as a boy.

But while Cobbett still admired his old job, he had scant regard for the guardians of the fields made of straw and ragged clothes. 'These shoy-hoys,' he wrote, 'exercise their

RURAL RIDES

IN THE SOUTHERN, WESTERN AND EASTERN COUNTIES
OF ENGLAND, TOGETHER WITH

TOURS IN SCOTLAND

AND IN THE NORTHERN AND MIDLAND COUNTIES OF
ENGLAND, AND

LETTERS FROM IRELAND

BY

WILLIAM COBBETT

THE WHOLE, INCLUDING MANY RIDES AND TOURS
NEVER BEFORE REPRINTED, EDITED WITH AN INTRO-
DUCTION, NOTES, A BIOGRAPHICAL RECORD OF UPWARDS
OF NINE HUNDRED PERSONS MENTIONED, AN INDEX OF
PLACES, AND A BIBLIOGRAPHICAL NOTE

BY

G. D. H. AND MARGARET COLE

WITH NUMEROUS VIGNETTES BY JOHN NASH, AND
A MAP OF COBBETT'S COUNTRY BY A. E. TAYLOR

VOLUME III

LONDON: PETER DAVIES
1930

A recent edition of William Cobbett's classic work, *Rural Rides*, complete
with a scarecrow illustration

influence but for a very short space of time. The birds quickly perceive that their guardianship of the treasures of the farmer is mere sham; and, like the sparrows in my neighbour's garden at Botley, they will, in a short time, make the top of the hat of a shoy-hoy a table whereon to enjoy the repast which they have purloined.'

Cobbett reserved his praise for the men and boys carrying out his old job for a column in his *Weekly Political Register* of 14 August 1819. Enthusing over the year's record harvest, he put this squarely down to the dedicated work of the bird-scarers, ' ... or, as we call them in Hampshire, Shoy-hoys'. He even named a few distinguished members of the fraternity: 'Look at the conduct of these shoy-hoys during the present season. The shoy-hoy Chamberlaine from Southampton, the shoy-hoy Palmer, and the two shoy-hoys from Nottingham. What vigil they kept, what terror they instilled into the bird population! No device of man is their equal!'

Would that there was more information on these redoubtable countrymen, but there is not.

Some of Cobbett's scepticism about the efficiency of the man-made scarecrow was shared by a contemporary, Henry Stephens (1790-1856), author of one of the first great works on modern farming methods, *The Book of the Farm*, first published in 1844 and reprinted constantly throughout the remainder of the century. Amidst voluminous entries on all manner of farming techniques and implements, Stephens has this to say in a chapter on 'Protecting Grain Harvests':

> *Scaring Birds.* Many devices have been tried to scare destructive birds from cornfields and green crops. The most common is the scarecrow. Scarecrows are made of various forms and materials, but the most common is the similitude of men and women in the tattered rags of beggars. Pieces of bright tin are made to flicker in the sunbeams, at the end of strings. Lines of white threads are hooked on from one object to another.
>
> But as soon as birds become familiarised with the form of these expedients, they lose their terrors. The contempt shown for them by birds has indeed already been told us by William Cobbett in his own quaint way.

Stephens then quotes Cobbett's passage about shoy-hoys reprinted above. His solution to the problem, he says, is for the harassed farmer to resort to his gun at regular intervals.

Two other writers of this time did not share this pessimism about the scarecrow: the prolific writer on the countryside Walter Thornbury (1828-76) and that great pioneer of the high adventure novel Sir Henry Rider Haggard (1856-1925).

Thornbury, a colourful and somewhat eccentric figure who lived for much of his life on a farm in Shropshire, was almost an advertisement for the scarecrow, for he had no fewer than five on his lands, all of which were re-dressed in new suits of clothing each year, three as men and two as women – or so one story about him claims: another version insists that passing tramps helping themselves to these clothes and leaving their rags behind were the real cause of the new fashions each season.

Be that as it may, Thornbury wrote about many aspects of country life in his books – in particular about old legends and superstitions, and a good many of the literary references to scarecrows discussed in Chapter 3 were extracted from his pages. Of scarecrows in general, though, he had this to say: 'To my mind the scarecrow is a feature of the landscape that is both a useful servant against the worst ravages of birds and a pleasure to look upon. Even the most humble, those that are no more than a bundle of sticks and a few rags, are a symbol of the passing seasons and, made in man's image, stand in our stead as silent observers of the glory of nature at work.'

Thornbury also uses the imagery of the scarecrow in his best-known book, *A Tour Round England* (1870), in which he followed Cobbett's footsteps across the country. Visiting Reading and inspecting the abbey, he has this to say: 'Perched on the tall flint tower of St Lawrence (a church once memorable for a silver gridiron containing a portion of the Saint), we remember that here Queen Elizabeth would attend service, looking sharply after the preacher's doctrine, from the canopied pew of the Knollys family. What a scarecrow to a blushing curate that stiff old lady in the ruff and jewelled stomacher must have been, glowering at him from under the bushy pyramid of her auburn hair!'

The young Cobbett, who worked as a 'human scarecrow', caricatured by James Gillray

Though Sir Henry Rider Haggard is famous all over the world for his novels, such as *King Solomon's Mines* and *She*, and for other stories about the great white hunter Allan Quatermain, he was also a dedicated countryman, living and farming for many years in his native Norfolk at All Hallows Farm. Indeed, he campaigned on behalf of better conditions for British farmers and wrote a book still highly regarded among agricultural works, *A Farmer's Year*, published in 1898. Employing his practised novelist's eye and very real knowledge of farming, Sir Henry presented a fascinating diary of life at the turn of the century on what was a typical English farm.

In an extract dated 4 February, he talks about the action he and his bailiff, a man named Hood, proposed to take against the birds threatening their crops. And what makes this item of particular interest is that the author theorizes a little as to why the use of scarecrows had declined at that time – as well as introducing another name for them:

> In walking round the farm this afternoon, I noticed that the rooks are playing havoc on the three acres of mixed grain which we drilled a few days ago for sheep food. They are congregated there literally by scores, and if you shout at them to frighten them away, they satisfy themselves by retiring to some trees near at hand and awaiting your departure to renew their operations. The beans attract them most, and their method of reducing these into possession is to walk down the line of the drill until (as I suppose) they smell a bean underneath. Then they bore down with their strong beaks and extract it, leaving a neat little hole to show that they have been there. Maize they love even better than beans; indeed, it is difficult to keep them off a field sown with that crop.
>
> Hood promises to set up some mawkins to frighten them, but the mawkin nowadays is a poor creature compared with what he used to be, and it is a wonder that any experienced rook consents to be scared by him. Thirty years or so ago he was really a work of art, with a hat, a coat, a stick, and sometimes a painted face, ferocious enough to frighten a little boy in the twilight, let alone a bird. Now a rag or two and a jumble-sale cloth cap are considered sufficient, backed up generally by the argument, which may prove more effective, of a dead rook tied up by the leg to a stick.

Henry P. Maskell (1870-1930), a most knowledgeable authority on rural matters, writing in *The English Countryman* of March 1905, tells a moral tale about the use of a dead bird tied to a stick as a deterrent to his fellows:

> Once upon a time a little boy, not yet past that happy age when every turning in life seems a path to wealth and fame, was studying *Robinson Crusoe*. He had just arrived at the page where the ripening ears in the castaway's cornfield were threatened with utter destruction by greedy, marauding bands

of wildfowl. Robinson, as usual, knew exactly what ought to be done. He fixed his gun, killed three of the feathered brigands, and hung them up like malefactors in chains as a warning to the rest. This procedure had a marvellous effect. The birds, terrified and conscience-striken, forsook all that part of the island, and never came near the cornfield as long as their dead brethren hung there.

Here was a notable discovery, and our young friend lost no time in applying it. Why should he not give his parents an agreeable surprise, and save them the expense of buying that large roll of wire netting which the gardener had requisitioned for the sweet peas? So an hour or two later, above the rows of tender green shoots there dangled three little dusky feathered corpses. One was a trapped blackbird, another a house sparrow shot with a catapult, the third was a chicken cut off prematurely by croup, for the boy had the instinct of the true naturalist and shrunk from taking life unnecessarily.

Alas for the best laid schemes of mice and men and little boys! From their hiding place in the greenhouse two surprised little eyes watched some scores of starlings hold a protracted coroner's inquest over the remains. The jury concluded the proceedings by dining on the three victims, of which they left nothing behind them but the beaks, and sweet peas formed the desert! Henceforth the adventures of Robinson Crusoe were relegated to a list of works which one young mind regarded as apocryphal in character!

Rider Haggard's reference to the 'mawkin' is one of many that give the other names that different areas of Britain have bestowed upon scarecrows.

After 'scarecrow' itself, the most widely used name is 'Jackalent'. The first printed reference to this occurs in Shakespeare's *The Merry Wives of Windsor* (1597), where Falstaff's mischievous young page, Robin, is sharply referred to as a 'little Jack-a-lent'.

The origin for this term is easily found in the OED, where, apart from describing a scarecrow, it can also mean 'a figure of a man set up to be pelted; an ancient form of the sport of "Aunt Sally" practised during Lent'. A more detailed account in Robert Chambers' *The Book of Days* (1863) under the heading for 10 February, Ash Wednesday reads:

The popular observances on Ash Wednesday are not of much

The scarecrow described as 'The Farmer's Friend' in a humorous illustration by the great George Cruickshank dated 1873

account. The cocks being now dispatched, a thin scare-crow like figure or puppet was set up, and shied at with sticks, an imitation of one of the sports of the preceding day. The figure was called a Jack-a-lent, a term which is often met with in old literature as expressive of a small and insignificant person. Beaumont and Fletcher, in one of their plays, make a character say –

> 'If I forfeit,
> Make me a Jack o'Lent and break my shins
> For untagged points and counters.'

Boys employed in the fields also used to go about clacking at doors, to get eggs or bits of bacon wherewith to make up a feast among themselves; and when refused, would stop the keyhole with dirt, and depart with a rhymed denunciation.

The use of the term jackalent for a scarecrow throughout many districts of England is confirmed by Arthur George ('A.G.') Street (1892-1966), farmer, author and broadcaster on radio and television. Writing in one of his innumerable books on country life, *Ditchampton Farm* (1946), about the family farm at Wilton near Salisbury in Wiltshire, where he grew up, Street said:

> I first heard the term jackalent when I was a lad working on the farm. One of my father's old labourers used it rather scathingly about a scarecrow I had made and was about to put up in a field of maize to keeps the crows off. Mind you, at first I thought he was talking about one of those fairy spirits called a 'Jack o'Lantern', until he offered me a dirty old piece of sacking from his pocket to make 'a real terrifyin' face on ee'm!'
>
> When I told my father about this he couldn't help laughing. I remember he also told me that jackalent could be used to describe an insignificant or contemptible person!

A.G. Street farmed at Ditchampton until he was eighteen and then emigrated to Canada, where he worked as a farm labourer until the outbreak of the First World War. In 1918, on the death of his father, he took over the family farm, and in 1931 he began to write the books that made him so popular with country-lovers – his knowledge of rural customs was truly encyclopedic.

In *Country Calendar* (1935) he claims that 'hodmadod'

was another word for scarecrow: 'The term was most used in Berkshire and on the Isle of Wight,' he explains, 'and in an old book, *Berkshire Glossary* published in 1888, I found it spelt Hodmedod and defined as "a scarecrow; usually a figure with a hat on, holding a stick to represent a gun".'

If Mr Street had looked further and consulted a companion volume, the *Isle of Wight Glossary* (1881), he would have seen that 'hodmadod' can also be used to describe a nondescript and even a deformed person. Perhaps because of this unfortunate association, it is much less heard today, though it appears in stories by Walter de la Mare and Nigel Kneale of *Quatermass* fame.

The autobiography of a farm labourer, *Brother to the Ox*, by Fred Kitchen (1940), explains another word for the scarecrow, a 'mammet'. Fred, who was born in the West Riding of Yorkshire and worked all his life on the land, mentions the term as being used when he was child by some of the older men in the district: 'I used to go collecting birds' eggs and more than once I was forced to run away from the pheasant keepers with the words "be off you young mammet" echoing at my back. They used it as a term of abuse, though I also heard it given to scarecrows.'

Fred Kitchen also cites the use of the expression in John Raymond's book *The Quiet Life* (1894): 'So Johnny conceived the idea of making a mammet with a pair of worn-out breeches, a discarded hunting coat and etc.'

In fact, 'mammet' can be traced not only in Yorkshire but also in Lancashire, while a derivation, 'murmet', is familiar in Devon and was first noted by that great regional novelist R.D. Blackmore in *Christowell* (1881), where he writes, 'Little Joe and me be like a pair of murmets.'

A further slight variation, mommet, is to be found in both Warwickshire and Worcestershire, in the former particularly applied to any 'odd figure', while in the latter it has even more sinister connotations – as a popular expression puts it: 'I'd as lif goo i' the night as the day, I amma afeared o' mommets.'

The same spelling has also been recorded in Somerset, whose *County Handbook* for the year 1903 quotes this anonymous request to a local householder: 'Can you please let us have a vew things, a old hat an' that, vor to make up a bit of a mommet, the rooks be rallin' in 'pon the taties?'

In the north of England and in Scotland, the terms 'tattie-doolies' and 'tattie-bogies' are both familiar as descriptions for scarecrows set up in potato fields to keep off birds. They are referred to in Sir Walter Scott's adventure story *Rob Roy* (1818), and several dictionaries note that 'tattie-bogie' can be applied to a ragged, unkempt or grotesquely dressed person. Apparently the words are also sometimes used in Scotland to refer to matted or tangled hair.

The final popular name is a 'mawkin', which Sir Henry Rider Haggard mentioned and which is common throughout all the East Anglian counties. Another famous author, Henry Williamson, who wrote that classic of wild life *Tarka the Otter* (1927), similarly spent several years running a farm in Norfolk, Old Castle Farm near Durston, and he has added to our knowledge about these scarecrows in his journal, *The Story of a Norfolk Farm* (1941).

'There were people about Old Castle Farm who believed that a mawkin would really help us,' he wrote. ' "We mun have a mawkin up to keep the birds off the line," one of my local helpers told me. Some of the Norfolk people called these scarecrows "old men" while others referred to them by the more traditional name of "Norfolk Mawkins".'

Though Williamson had his doubts about this belief, he knew better than to tempt nature any more than was necessary while he was learning to be a farmer, and so put up a rather impressive mawkin on the field called 'Twenty One Acres'. For his inspiration, he said, he had turned to the pages of a popular local book, *Son of the Fens* by David Emerson (1892), in which one of the characters observed, 'The Bayly's put sich a rar good mawkin i' the corn-leasow – anybody ood think it wuz a livin' mon!'

While travelling in the adjoining county of Suffolk, Williamson also heard a group of boys referring to some suits of clothes as mawkins ' ... because they had first been exhibited in a shop window on a model'. There was also, he said, a somewhat weird tradition among the people of this county to refer to any draped figure either alive *or* dead as a mawkin: 'More than once I heard a person referred to as looking "for all the world like a mawkin" and I never could restrain a little shudder at the mention.'

Another 'shudder-making' reference by Henry Williamson

The bold-looking mawkin of Old Castle Farm described by Henry Williamson in his book, *The Story of a Norfolk Farm* (1941)

tells of a human scarecrow who was said to have sold his soul to the Devil in return for supernatural powers. The man, known as Jack o'Kent, was said to have worked his mastery over nature, the elements and even evil spirits on the borders of Herefordshire and Monmouthshire at some time during the Middle Ages – the story providing more evidence of just how long the human scarecrow had been employed.

In an article, 'Wizardry on the Welsh Border', in *Folklore* Magazine, number 43, 1932, B.A. Wherry wrote:

> Once Jack was engaged by a farmer to scare crows, but there was a fair going on in the town and Jack didn't mean to miss it, so he called all the crows together from all the fields around, and when they were all collected, he sent them into an old barn, with no roof to it. But Jack put the crows in there and said something to them, and they couldn't get out, try as they might.
>
> So Jack, he went to the fair, but when he had been enjoying himself there a bit, he met his master. So the farmer said, 'Hullo, Jack, what art doin' here? Didn't I tell thee to look after th' crows?' But Jack says, 'T' crows be all right, master.' And he took his master to the old barn, and sure enough there was the crows, and they couldn't get out, although that barn had no roof, until Jack told them to.

There is a very similar version of this story told of a Radnorshire wizard called Davies, but equally there are other less fanciful accounts of human scarecrows which confirms the effectiveness, if not the magical capabilities, of the profession.

First, a general overview of the occupation provided by historian Roy Palmer in his book *The Folklore of Warwickshire* (1976), which mirrors what has happened in other parts of Britain:

> Germinating seeds were protected by children stationed in the fields for long hours armed with rattles or clappers. 'I was a youngster of nine when I began to earn money,' wrote Joseph Arch, who was born at Barford in 1826. 'My first job was crow-scaring, and for this I received fourpence a day. This day was a twelve hour one, so it sometimes happened that I got more than was in the bargain, and that was a smart taste of

the farmer's stick when he ran across me outside the field I had been set to watch.' Joseph Ashby of Tysoe, who was born in 1859, also started work as a bird-scarer at the age of nine. To cheer his loneliness he 'took to shouting so as to hear a human voice. This method had another convenience; you couldn't cry while you shouted.'

According to Roy Palmer, these bird-scarers had a number of songs and rhymes that they sang to while away the hours. One such, which he collected in Ilmington, runs:

> Ye pigeons and crows, away! away!
> Why do you steal my master's tay? [tea]
> If he should come with his long gun,
> You must fly and I must run!

Many villages had different versions of this, says Palmer, citing another example from the appropriately named hamlet of Shottery:

> Shoo-hoo, shoo-hoo!
> Away, birds, away,
> Tek a corn
> And leave a corn
> And come no more ter-day.

A third tune was apparently a particular favourite of the more violently natured boys:

> Cooo-oo!
> I've got a pair of clappers,
> And I'll knock e' down back'ards;
> I've got a great stone,
> And I'll break your backbone.

A personal view of the life of the human scarecrow is offered by the Sussex countryman writer Bob Copper in his book *A Song For Every Season* (1975), in which he tells of the work of the 'animated scarecrows' – as he calls them – from the viewpoint of having once belonged to the fraternity himself. Talking about the 'annual hazard' of the 'five or six

Nineteenth-century sketch of a young bird-scarer

hundred sooty, ragged-winged robbers from the rookery in the neighbouring village' who would fly down to steal the newly scattered corn, he writes:

> To combat this very real threat to the crops, labourers, mostly the older men, and boys, were sent into the fields bird-scaring, or 'rook starving' as they called it, and they used home-made pairs of clappers that rattled and clapped when shaken violently. These were made of a bat-shaped piece of wood – rather like a butter-pat – with two loose pieces of board wired on either side to form clappers. They were most effective when first used in the mornings, but as time went on the rooks seemed to notice that, though a volley of what they first took to be gunfire rattled out at regular intervals, neither they nor

any of their companions suffered any casualties. They presumably concluded that either the bird-scarer was a singularly bad marksman or, clever birds, that it was not gunfire at all.

In any event, they gradually grew bolder and merely flapped languidly into the air in token recognition of the bird-scarer's efforts and then, after a brief circular flight, returned to their foraging with renewed vigour. This state of affairs developed until finally, clap as he may, the frustrated bird-scarer could do no more than induce only those birds in the immediate vicinity to leave the ground. To overcome this difficulty one man walked around with a shot-gun and from time to time a well-aimed charge would remind the rooks of the dangers of complacency and lend renewed significance to the sound of the clappers.

One such gun-man, relating how on his rounds he had fired both barrels of his gun at a flock of starlings that went flying overhead, concluded his story, 'But I didn't git ne'er one an 'em. I reck'n I must've aimed a liddle low, 'cos over in the next fiel' I picked up 'alf a bushel of legs!'

Also in his narrative, Bob Copper describes another method employed by this determined band in the war to save the corn: 'To make fuller use of the presence in the fields of these animated scarecrows, as they might be called without disrespect, for this is written by one of that ancient fraternity – they would sometimes be set on flint picking, which was a never-ending job on the shallow, flinty top-soil of the down-lands. Every heavy shower of rain brought a new outcrop of flints to the surface of a field where the soil had been washed away, and one or two of the older men were firmly convinced that the flints grew like any other crop, not only in numbers but in size! Leastways, these might be hurled at those birds most reluctant to quit their foraging.

Closing on a more personal note, Bob Copper reminisces about his own introduction to the business of being a human scarecrow:

When Grand-dad was very old and crippled with rheumatics, bird-scaring was one of the few jobs he could still manage. They used to take him out in a horse and cart and sit him in the middle of a field in his favourite chair with his muzzle-loader gun, a pair of clappers, a jar of beer and his bread and cheese tied up in a red and white spotted handkerchief. There he would sit all day long until they came to pick him up at tea time.

After all those years of riding round these same lands on his cob, bearing on his shoulders the full responsibility of a farm of that size, with its 1,000 acres of arable land and over fifty employees, he accepted without resentment that age and the 'screws' had brought him, in his retirement, to this the most menial of tasks on the farm. He was not even paid for it but he was amply rewarded by the knowledge that in spite of his physical incapacity he was still doing a worthwhile job.

I was only about five at the time but sometimes I was allowed to go along with him with a miniature pair of clappers that Dad had made for me, because I was not 'man enough' to handle a full-size pair. Whenever Grand-dad shot a rook I had to run and fetch it to him and he would tie it on to a thatching-rod and make me stick it into the ground some distance away. Here the unfortunate bird would swing from its gibbet as a grim reminder to those that got away.

Full of insights though Bob Copper's account is, he cannot match the colourful and moving account of the life of a human scarecrow which appeared in the *Daily Mail* of 11 April 1908. This report, written by E. Clephan Palmer and headed 'The Scarecrow: A Brave Old Age', offers a very special insight into the life of an old countryman the like of whom we shall probably never see again.

As he stands out there, in the middle of the flat Suffolk field, there is little to show he is not the ordinary, inanimate scarecrow. He stands motionless for five minutes at a time, and only when a bird is tempted by the fresh corn just appearing above the ground does he show any sign of life.

From the road outside the field he looks exactly like the conventional collection of old clothes propped upon a stick. The ragged overcoat and the misshapen hat can be seen any day, at this time of the year, in almost any field in England. Even the rooks are contemptuous of the figure, and every now and then a number of them appear leisurely above the hedge and settle on the field.

But then it is that the scarecrow moves; he hits an old tin can with the rusty handle of a shovel and frightens the birds, and makes them fly quickly out of sight. So he spends his day,

Youngster at work as a bird-scarer in the film *Captain Clegg* (1962)

this old man, and at the end he is paid eighteen pence. He is the village scarecrow.

Every morning now, soon after the light comes, he leaves his son's cottage in the meadow and walks through the village street to the fields a mile away. And then, for nearly twelve hours, he keeps the birds from the corn by making a noise on his old tin can. Whatever the weather may be, he is expected to be there. In rain he may shelter under the nearest hedge, but he must watch his fields, and if the birds take advantage of his absence he must go into the open and scare them from the corn.

For this old man knows well that he is competing for his living against the clothes propped upon a stick, or the dead rooks scattered about the field, and it is necessary that he should take a certain pride in his profession. Unless he can show the farmer that he is more effective than the conventional scarecrow, he cannot make a living in the few months between the sowing of the seed and the appearance of the corn.

Fortunately for him he need not fear competition with the boys of the village. The days when they were willing to earn sixpence by frightening birds from the fields have gone. In his day – that is, when he was young – anyone in the village who was under twelve was glad to earn a penny a day pocket money and five pence for the home. But now there are the schools, and the towns close by, and the railway to London.

So it is that he has almost a monopoly in his profession. While the boys of the village are in school he can earn enough in these few months of the year to keep him from the workhouse. He is still capable of scaring birds. His very clothes are a qualification. He looks exactly like a scarecrow, and he has the advantage of being able to hit an old tin can with the rusty handle of a shovel.

At one o'clock he has his dinner of bread and cheese by the side of the hedge, but every now and then he gets up and looks round to see that the fields are free from birds. Sometimes, when the day is colder than usual, his granddaughter from the cottage a mile away brings him a hot dinner in a basin covered with a cloth, and while he eats she talks to him about her school, and if a bird appears runs carefully on to the field and claps her hands and frightens it. And when the dinner is finished, she gaily says, 'Good-bye', and goes back along the road. And then the old man – this shabby guardian of the fields – is left alone. For the fields now are empty of everything except the growing corn. As far as the eye can see there is nothing except the flat, bare land, cut into odd shapes by hedges and by roads.

The only suggestion of life is a collection of old clothes propped upon a stick in a field nearly a mile away. And when the old man looks at this silent competitor of his he is filled with new energy, and strides about the field, making a great noise with his old tin can.

He did not always earn his living in this way. By the time he was ten he was apprenticed to the fields, and proudly led the horses while a man held the plough. And soon he became a carter, and then, himself, a ploughman. And so skilful was he that he won many prizes at competitions; and twenty years ago he was famous in his county as a ploughman.

All the younger men of the farm were put under his charge, and he it was who taught them the subtle inflections of 'Whoa,

Boxer!' and 'Come round, Schmiler!'. No one in this district, it is said there to this day, had so perfect a control of horses, and ploughmen from other farms came to look at his furrows and to ask him why they were so straight and clean. Not until he was nearly seventy did his hand and eye and voice lose their cunning, and then, when he found that his horses took so little notice of him and that his furrows were no longer straight, he stopped at once from a certain pride, and did instead odd jobs about the farm.

Then his wife died, and he thought wearily of the workhouse; but the son to whom he had given the secrets of his ploughing went with his young wife to the thatched cottage where he was a boy, and together they persuaded the old man to come and live with them. There for the last ten years he had lived quite happily and been something of an oracle in the village. So long as there is an odd job for him to do he is content. Only idleness makes him unhappy. He is satisfied to watch his son take his old place at the plough, and to wait till the seed is sown, so that he may earn a little money by scaring birds.

He is not ashamed of being a scarecrow. He enjoys the long day in the fields on which he has spent his life. He knows every inch of them. For forty years he ploughed them, as no other man could, and he is glad, in this brave old age of his, not to lose sight of them.

He makes jokes about his new profession, and no one wants to sneer at him. For although he is the village scarecrow, he is also the village favourite, and there is not a man or woman or child in the place who would willingly let him go from them. As he walks through the village on these cold spring mornings, carrying his tin can and the rusty handle of a shovel, everyone who is about says, 'Good morning' to him, and children tell him they are coming out to help him after school.

The one thing he regrets is that he has as a competitor only the collection of old clothes propped upon a stick, or the dead rooks scattered about the field a mile away.

Heart-tugging as this story must have seemed to the *Mail*'s readers back in 1908, it seems doubly so today – that an old man after a lifetime of service still found it necessary to work in order to sustain himself, even if he *was* the stalwart kind of soul who preferred to be doing something rather than sitting inactive at home.

"I started life at the age of seven as bird-scarer on a farm, but I never made much of a success at it."

An inimitable *Punch* comment on the job of bird-scaring from the issue of 8 May 1940

Though there is no clue as to the identity of this human scarecrow, the location of the story is given as Suffolk, and several old Suffolk farmhands can still recall stories of human scarecrows like this aged hero – one man even suggests he might have been a once-famous ploughman from the pretty village of Nayland called Charlie Smith, but that is only speculation.

There is an intriguing recent sequel to this story, provided once again by the *Daily Mail*. Its issue of 16 May 1985 ran a story headlined 'Want to be a Worzel?' and reported, 'Fruit farmer Eddie Waltham is offering unemployed teenagers in Birmingham – where he once worked – £50 per week jobs as "live" scarecrows to keep birds off his cherry orchards near Rochester, Kent.'

Two days later the *Mail* carried a second story under the headline 'Worzels Galore': 'Farm manager Eddie Waltham of Rochester, Kent, has chosen five budding Worzel Gummidges from the 100 boys who applied to spend a month as human scarecrows in his orchard for £50 a week.'

Doubtless the old ploughman of E. Clephan Palmer's story would have been amazed at the wage his old job now commanded – but he would surely have allowed himself to enjoy the report which a *Mail*'s journalist, John Passmore, sent from Kent on 22 May, bearing the headline 'Stone the Crows, It's Alive and Rattling!'

> The starling was so surprised, it almost fell out of the sky. It wasn't used to scarecrows running ... or shouting. And life in the cherry orchard would never be quite the same again.
>
> The scarecrows at Buckhole Farm in Kent actually are alive. They wave football rattles and their voices have been tuned on the terraces at Birmingham City. Farmer Eddie Waltham, standing there with his dog at his heel and watching Steve Stirling and his three mates from the city attacking the first job in their lives, was a happy man. 'They're marvellous,' he said. 'Better than I ever hoped.'
>
> Mr Waltham's farm comprises ten acres of prize-winning cherries worth around £20,000. But his land just happens to be bounded on three sides by the Northwood Bird Sanctuary at High Halstow. Finches abound. And to a finch, a plump young cherry is the equivalent of Kentucky Fried Chicken. And that, according to farmer Waltham, is where the human scarecrows come in.
>
> 'I don't like shooting birds and they get used to a gas cannon which goes off at regular intervals. I won't have chemicals, nets are cruel because the birds get caught in them, and the idea of hanging dead birds in a tree to scare off the living ones absolutely sickens me,' he said.
>
> The only answer, it seemed, was human scarecrows. And, as he says, 'Most of all, I like this solution because it gives these lads a job.' Farmer Waltham says he's been unemployed himself and knows how it feels. He also knows that a month's work won't cure everything. But he said, 'If these lads prove they can stick to a job that involves getting up at three in the morning, that's a pretty good qualification for anything!'

This is not the only instance in recent years where the job of human scarecrow has been revived. In 1980 former professional football player Phil Turner of Rhyl in Clwyd got

Modern bird-scarers: the youngsters employed by Kent orchard owner, Eddie Waltham, to protect his cherry trees in 1985

ten job offers when he advertised himself in his local paper as a 'first-class scarecrow looking for work – has own suit'. And in 1986 another cherry farmer in Oxfordshire, James Best, taking a leaf from the book of his colleague in Kent, picked two boys and a girl from a sackful of applications to his advertisement for scarers to keep hungry birds out of his forty-six acres of orchards. The three students still found that tramping the farm from dawn to dusk was exhausting work – even if inflation had hiked up their wages to £100 a week.

The conclusion, then, to be drawn from these reports of human scarers pacing the fields, not to mention scarecrows still being made, is that the scarecrow is very much a part of the rural scene. But questions remain unanswered as to just how he first got there and what factors led to his creation and development. There are three possible answers.

A HISTORY OF THE MAWKIN

A convenient point at which to begin the enquiry is with the type of bird-scarer which is most easy to explain – that of the dead bird hung on the branch of a tree or attached to a stake in the ground, there to act as a deterrent to its fellows. This has for many centuries been regarded in the country as an infallible threat – though sceptics will quickly point out that there is ample evidence of the indifference with which animals treat the death of their own kind, even their own mates and offspring, unless their protective instinct has been aroused at the actual moment of tragedy. So how did this curious belief begin?

Philology and folk lore claim that superstition is just one of the survivals from the ancient times when our ancestors believed themselves to be surrounded by evil supernatural beings who could be propitiated only by a live sacrifice. As civilization progressed, so the nature of the sacrifice changed: when life itself became regarded as sacred, an animal was substituted.

The ancient tradition of protecting crops by nailing a dead bird in the vicinity – as sketched by David Collins

With the advent of Christianity came a God who loved and blessed all His creations and demanded no such ritual slaughter. But though this religion to a large extent eclipsed that of evil spirits, man could not altogether abandon a certain sneaking dread of them, and many of the old observances lived on just beneath the surface of life under the categorization of 'superstitions'. Now at last, though, evil spirits could be satisfied with the simplest and most harmless of 'sacrifices'.

Thus the first theory of the origin of the scarecrow is that it may have started out as a sacrifice to Nature.

We have seen that the jackalent was originally a sort of puppet-like figure at which, during Lent, people hurled sticks; prior to this, it was cocks that were the object of these attacks. So is it not possible to argue that perhaps in pagan days man was done to death in this manner and then set up in the fields as an offering? Might not this be the reason why in Normandy and Brittany – where Druidical rites were once prevalent and where legends about them survive in abundance – a life-size effigy of Christ on the cross is set amidst the corn each year? It could be surmised from this that the Church had sought to turn its people from the barbaric custom of slaughtering a real man by providing an alternative which was an all-sufficient sacrifice.

Support for this argument is to be found in the writings of Henry P. Maskell, one of whose essays, 'Scarecrows' in *The Treasury* of June 1906, adds another factor to the discussion:

> The strongest argument of all in favour of considering the scarecrow a sacrifice to the powers of the wind and the storm and the hail, rather than the means of driving away undesirable intruders, is the fact generally admitted that it is for the latter purpose a comparative failure. Set in a pear tree, for example, it might serve its turn. All birds respect the man who climbs the tree. He is above ordinary men, maybe a half-developed bird who might at any moment proceed to take to himself wings and fly in pursuit of them.
>
> In the cornfield it is another matter. Whole meal wheat is good brain food and develops the faculties for inductive reasoning amazingly. Not that rooks and starlings will venture on such a supreme analytical test as the impudent sparrow who builds a nest in the scarecrow's hat, with materials torn out of his innards! But what bird cares about a man standing stock still on the ground? And such a man! He cannot be the owner of the farm, or he would not idle his time away when there was weeding and hoeing to do.

'No man except a positive idiot would stand still like that in pelting rain and baking sunshine alike. Besides, that shocking bad hat and tattered coat can only belong to a tramp, a trespasser like themselves. And so they fall to and ignore the odd creature's presence.

Though Maskell considers the scarecrow 'a fine old English institution', he is none the less firmly convinced the figure has been 'going steadily down-hill in the social scale from prehistoric times'. Yet, he adds:

If birth and ancestry are to be regarded, I believe the scarecrow can point to a very glorious past. Perchance his ancient honours were even more august than those that I have suggested for him – for some contend that he was not merely an offering to the gods, but was an image of the Deity himself, some Celtic Apollo, or Ceres, or Terminus – and, as such, received divine honours. All the adversities and indignities that have befallen him in these latter days he has endured in the highest possible spirit.

No one could meet misfortune more philosophically than he does; even when overthrown and treated with contumely he was never heard to utter a complaint. What truer mark of a great mind than to meet injury and ingratitude without being stung into a display of resentment!

There is, however, no evidence to support Maskell's suggestion of a divine origin for the scarecrow, though over the years his kind have certainly stood on the lands of the very foremost kings and monarchs.

The second theory as to the scarecrow's origin gives it a much more humble birth. The redoubtable researcher W.O.G. Lofts believes the clues to its creation can be found in another of its names, 'mawkin':

Apart from describing a scarecrow the word is also of considerable antiquity and can refer to the bundle of rags fastened on a pole which bakers used for centuries to clean out their brick ovens before putting in the bread.

Now corn was very essential to these men, and I believe they used to take their spare 'mawkins' after they had finished with them and plant them in the ground where the seeds were growing. You can imagine they looked rather like thin human beings, and when the wind was up the rags would blow and flutter in the air scaring off the birds.

There is some evidence to give weight to this contention in the books of a handful of writers on country life. Paul Bobbin, for example, in his *Sequel* (1819), notes: 'Tum o'Williums took up 'e the baker's Mokin [another spelling of mawkin] and put em in the field for to scare off they birds.' John Jackson, in *Southward Ho* (1894), quotes an old farm labourer as saying, 'Dere wos a law chep as wur a bit ov a nabbler an a live mawkin wot hed awves looked as if 'e'd a bin fresh pulled from groun'.' And the Yorkshire writer Tom Treddlehoyle, in *Bairnsla Ann* (1847), describes a scarecrow-thin character in his story 'as wor as black as a baker's maukin' (another variation of the word).

Corn figures in a straw dance to celebrate a successful harvest

The third suggestion as to the scarecrow's origin is perhaps the most intriguing of all. It was proposed to me by a distinguished member of the Folklore Society, Dr Jacqueline Simpson, author of several major books about folklore and mythology, who was very generous with her time and knowledge while I was researching this history. In a letter to me of March 1987 she wrote: 'I suppose that in an indirect sort of way one could claim that an ugly/aggressive figure or symbol which drives away evil magical forces is a sort of ancestor to the scarecrow's more practical functions.'

But it was in the context of making jackalents that Dr Simpson advanced the most interesting theory.

> They, of course, originated in those medieval customs of making an ugly, thin, tattered figure to represent Lent in the context of carnival customs. These in turn have links with the custom (copiously discussed in Sir James Frazer's *The Golden Bough*, 1890) of making, parading and destroying a puppet representing Winter and Death at some Spring date, i.e. Shrove Tuesday, Mid Lent Sunday, Easter. This still (or recently) survived in Eastern Europe – for the picture researcher who assisted me on my latest book, *European Mythology*, got a lovely photograph of Polish girls doing it in 1966, and another of Hungarian women dressing up a death-puppet at a fairly recent date, though the actual year wasn't specified.
>
> In a sense, I suppose *any* ugly puppet could be considered analogous to a scarecrow, but, frustratingly, it seems almost impossible to find examples of puppets being used to protect crops. However, I did find the following in an article on 'Estonian Mythology' by Jonas Balys in Funk & Wagnall's *Dictionary of Folklore, Mythology and Legend:* 'Estonians also have various idols formed by the hand of man. Seventeenth century sources frequently mention the Metsik, which at the time of the New Year and Shrove Tuesday was formed from straw in the shape of a man or woman and put on a tree or fence. The idol was to protect cattle against wild beasts and also to promote the fertility of crops.'
>
> This, I think, one could plausibly call a type of scarecrow.

But *is* it the answer to our question? *Did* the scarecrow therefore originate as a fertility symbol to help promote the growth of the seeds in the ground rather than as a device for scaring off birds? Dr Simpson writes:

> I had hoped to find some evidence that the innumerable Corn Spirits (Rye Hag, Corn Wolf etc – see *The Golden Bough*) which were so frequently represented by straw/wheat images

made at harvest time were displayed *in the fields* as protectors. But no! Invariably they are either taken *into the farm or barn* and kept for luck until next year, or are used as a taunt against slower harvesters by tossing them onto the latter's land. So, regrettably, one must conclude that the Corn Dolly figures do not perform the functions of a scarecrow.

But what makes this rather odd is that that Corn Spirits, whether in human or animal form, were often imagined and said to be lurking among the growing crops to protect them from children and trespassers, and functioned as imaginary bogies to scare them off. One would think it a logical next step to put a figure in the field and say, 'Look, children, that's the Rye Hag (or whatever) – She'll eat you if you go too close!' But I have not found even one shred of evidence for this.

So the case for this origin of the scarecrow ends so tantalizingly close to a solution that it may well be nearest the truth. If records or witnesses can be found who could recall being made to *fear* scarecrows when they were children, we shall be even closer. A definite link between the bogy-figure

The effect of the 'ugly figure': a George Cruickshank engraving of a scarecrow frightening a late-night passer-by

and the scarecrow – beyond that mentioned in the *OED* – would be of paramount importance.

As it is, the creation of the first scarecrow must remain for the time being still a mystery – which is perhaps only as it should be, for he has always been something of an enigma. In that very fact, surely, lies much of the reason for our fascination with him. In all the best mysteries a complete answer invariably devalues and even demeans the central figure. So it would be with the scarecrow.

3   The Scarecrow in Literature

'No eye hath seen such scarecrows.'

WILLIAM SHAKESPEARE

The scarecrow has featured in English literature a great deal more than is probably generally realized. No doubt L. Frank Baum's classic story of the scarecrow in search of a brain in *The Wonderful Wizard of Oz* is familiar to the reader, as perhaps also Nathaniel Hawthorne's tale of the scarecrow brought to life in 'Feathertop' and the famous Worzel Gummidge created by Barbara Euphan Todd, but what of Kenneth Grahame's leering member of the fraternity found in 'An Autumn Encounter', Walter de la Mare's poetic figure in 'The Scarecrow', or even Clemence Dane's sinister scarecrow who is the subject of her novel *The Arrogant History of White Ben*?

The very earliest reference to the scarecrow in a work of fiction occurred in the verse story *The Faerie Queen* by Edmund Spenser (1552-99), published in 1590. Spenser wrote much of this tale of courtly romance while living on the rich lands of Kilcolman Castle in Cork, and it was at the instigation of his neighbour, the courtier and navigator Sir Walter Raleigh – one of the people to whom the work was dedicated – that Spenser took the manuscript to England, first presenting it to Queen Elizabeth and then supervising its very successful publication. The reference to a scarecrow occurs in Book II, Canto 3, when the valiant Sir Guyon, seeking the murderers of his parents, draws his sword on a scruffy figure he suddenly encounters on a wayside bank:

> Thereat the scarecrow wexed wondrous prowd,
> Through fortune of his first adventure fayre,

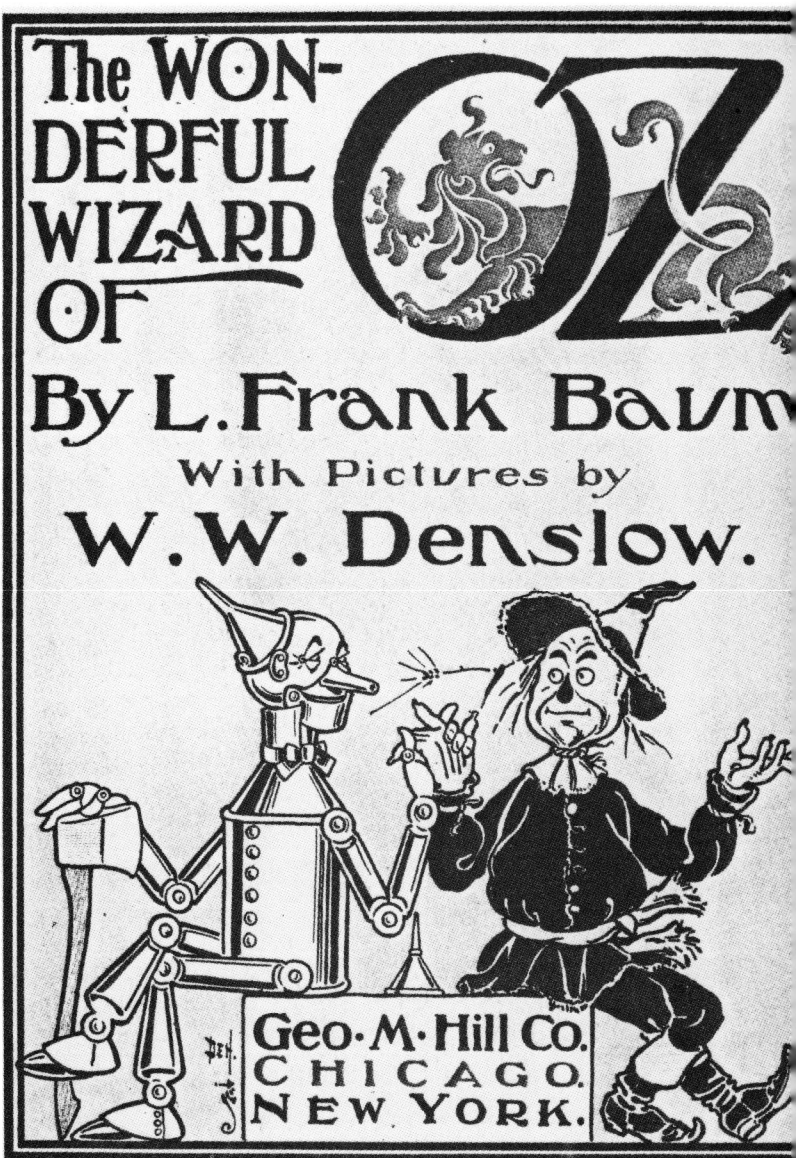

The most famous scarecrow in literature from Frank Baum's *The Wonderful Wizard of Oz*: as originally sketched by W.W. Denslow for the first edition of the book in 1900

And with big thundering voice revyld him lowd;
  'Vile caytive, vassal of dread and despayre?
Unworthie of the commune breathed ayre,
Why livest thou, dead dog, a lenger day,
And does not unto death thyselfe prepayre?'

Happily, despite this abrasive encounter, the 'scarecrow' and Sir Guyon make friends, the stranger becoming the nobleman's servant.

Spenser's friend Sir Walter Raleigh came from an ancient farming family in Devon, and it is said that he used scarecrows to protect the first crops of potatoes and tobacco he brought back from America and planted on his 42,000 acres estate in Munster. He alluded to scarecrows in his book *A Discourse of War* (1616), drawing a somewhat unusual comparison between them and weapons of warfare: 'Many of those great guns,' he wrote, 'wanting powder and shot, stood but as cyphers and scarecrows.'

William Shakespeare (1564-1616) refers to the scarecrow in no fewer than four of his works, *Henry VI, Part One* (1591), *Henry IV, Part One* (1597), *The Merry Wives of Windsor* (1597), and *Measure for Measure* (1604).

In the first part of *Henry VI*, the scarecrow appears in a speech by Lord Talbot, who has recently returned to London after being released from captivity in the hands of the French. Asked how he was treated as a prisoner, Talbot says (Act I, Scene 3):

With scoffs, and scorns, and contumelious taunts.
In open market-place produced they me,
To be a public spectacle to all:
Here, said they, is the terror of the French,
The scare-crow that affrights our children so!

That colourful character Sir John Falstaff makes the second of Shakespeare's references to scarecrows (*Henry IV*, Part I, Act IV, Scene 2). Debating with himself about the ragged army of recruits he has raised for the King's service while on the way to Coventry, he declares: 'A mad fellow met me on the way, and told me I had unloaded all the gibbets and pressed the dead bodies. No eye hath seen such scarecrows. I'll not march through Coventry with them, that's flat!'

Falstaff again mentions scarecrows in the comedy *The Merry Wives of Windsor*. This time, however, it is his trio of assistants, the 'irregular humourists' Bardolph, Pistol and Nym, whom he refers to as resembling scarecrows in both their dress and manners.

Perhaps more interesting in this work is Shakespeare's use of another word for a scarecrow, a jackalent. It occurs in Act III, Scene 3 in connection with Falstaff's slippery young servant, Robin, who after informing the Mistresses Ford and Page that Sir John has come surreptitiously calling at their back door, is chided accusingly by Mistress Page: 'You little Jack-a-lent, have you been true to us?'

And when Falstaff appears before the ladies, he draws a similar comparison when speaking of how he has been made a fool of: 'See now,' he says, 'how wit may be made a Jack-a-lent when 'tis upon ill employment!'

In Act II, Scene I of *Measure for Measure*, written seven years later, Shakespeare has Angelo, the deputy to Duke Vincentio, declare:

William Shakespeare – the man who immortalized the scarecrow

THE SCARECROW IN LITERATURE

We must not make a scarecrow of the law,
Setting it up to fear the birds of prey,
And let it keep one shape, till custom make it
Their perch, and not their terror.

Two of Shakespeare's contemporaries in the theatre, the playwright partnership of Francis Beaumont (1584-1616) and John Fletcher (1579-1625) made mention of the scarecrow in two of their London productions.

They first referred to scarecrows in *Bonduca*, produced in 1619. This historical drama about the life of the first-century British Warrior Queen Bonduca (better known as Boadicea) was set primarily in her kingdom, covering the part of East Anglia now occupied by Norfolk and Suffolk, scene of her battles with the invading Romans. In discussing the men who have been gathered from Bonduca's kingdom to take on the Romans, Hengo, the Warrior Queen's nephew, enquires:

Can these fight? They look
Like empty scabbards all, no mettle in 'em;
Like men of clouts, set to keep crows from orchards:
Why, I dare fight with these!

The play also contains another interesting reference to a scarecrow – 'set up in a pear tree that it might serve its turn', the inference being that these figures were believed to keep birds out of fruit trees as well as off fields.

Beaumont and Fletcher's *The Wild-Goose Chase*, first staged in 1621, concerned a fleet-of-foot seducer named Mirabel the Wild-Goose who is finally outmanoeuvred into marriage by his long-suffering fiancée, Oriana. Along the way, Mirabel breaks many a female heart, including that of Lillia, who despairingly says:

Name him no more;
For, though I long for a husband, I hate him
And would be married sooner to a monkey,
Or to a Jack of Straw, than such a juggler.

Ben Jonson (1572-1637), the patron of Beaumont and Fletcher, also referred to scarecrows twice in his works. In *The Staple of Newes*, first performed in 1625, the Canter, Peni-Boy, speaks of his wayward son and his attitude to soldiering:

> This is a moth, a rascall, a Court-rat,
> That gnawes the common-wealth with broking suits,
> And eating grievances! So, a *true Souldier*,
> He is his *Countryes strength*, his *Soveraignes safety*,
> And to secure his peace, he makes himself
> The *heyre* of danger, nay the *subject* of it,
> And runnes those vertuous hazards, that this Scarre-crow
> Cannot endure to heare of!

In his later and more famous work, *Tale of a Tub* (1633), Act IV, Scene 3, Jonson refers to the ancient custom of playing a jackalent on Ash Wednesday: 'Thou travell'dst to Hampstead Heath on Ash Wednesday,' the narrator affirms to a man he has encountered, 'where thou didst stand six weeks the Jack of Lent for boys to hurl, three throws a penny, at thee.'

The eighteenth century saw the first sustained piece of humour about the scarecrow, in one of the contributions of the essayist Joseph Addison (1672-1719) to the famous magazine *The Spectator*, Addison in the March issue of 1711, wrote about the sociability of man and how he ' ... takes all Occasions and Pretences of forming himself into those little Nocturnal Assemblies which are commonly known by the name of *Clubs*'.

Addison writes first of the 'Club of Fat Men' located in what he calls a considerable market town, to which those of huge bulk are admitted. Only men who cannot squeeze through a passage-way and have to use special folding doors to get in are granted membership, he says. He then continues with details of the 'Scare-Crows and Skeletons Club':

'In opposition to this Society, there sprung up another composed of Scare-Crows and Skeletons, who being very meagre and envious, did all they could to thwart the Designs of their Bulky Brethren, whom they represented as Men of

Robinson Crusoe had a memorable, and successful, encounter with the birds threatening his precious crops in Daniel Defoe's classic novel

Dangerous Principles; till at length they worked them out of the Favour of the People, and consequently out of the Magistracy. These Factions tore the Corporation in Pieces for several Years, till at length they came to this Accommodation; that the two Bailiffs of the Town should be annually chosen out of the two Clubs; by which means the principal Magistrates are at this day coupled like Rabbits, one fat and one lean!'

Daniel Defoe (1660-1731) wrote of the scarecrow in two quite dissimilar works. In *Robinson Crusoe* (1719), his undisputed masterpiece, there is a scene where the castaway discovers his ripening ears of corn being threatened by the island's greedy birds and turns to a time-honoured method to protect this precious harvest. Having killed three birds, ' ... I took them up, and served them as we serve notorious thieves in England, viz., hanged them in chains, for a terror to others. It is impossible to imagine almost that this should have had such an effect as it had, for the fowls would not only not come at the corn, but, in short, they forsook all that part of the island, and I could never see a bird near the place as long as my scarecrows hung there.'

Henry Maskell, writing in *The Treasury* magazine of June 1906, confirmed Defoe's story:

> The episode in *Robinson Crusoe* is no cockney invention. Daniel Defoe was a wideawake conscientious observer of men and things; he never wrote a line which he was not prepared to defend by chapter and verse. Crusoe was a Yorkshire man. To this day in the West Riding a dead hare or rabbit is frequently to be seen hung in the hedge where the track of these animals enters a field. On enquiring the reason, some bumpkin will assure you that his cabbage patch is protected by an infallible taboo. All over rural England some like notices will be found in existence. The gamekeeper who shoots a stoat or weasel hangs it up on the nearest tree; the barn wall serves as a Newgate Calendar decorated with nailed up skeletons of hawks, magpies, rats and owls. It is a devout belief that these pests of the farmyard will see it and fear.

Defoe used the association of fear and the scarecrow in his later philosophical tome *The Modern History of the Devil*, published in 1726. In this 'revelation' of the Devil's 'more private Conduct down to the Present time', he writes (in Part II Chapter 3) 'Of the manner of Satan's acting and carrying on his affairs in this world' and states: 'Nor, indeed, should we have much reason to be frightened at him, or at least none of those silly things could be said of him which we now amuse ourselves about, and by which we set him up like a scarecrow to frighten children and old women, to fill up old stories, make songs and ballads, and, in a word, carry on the low-prized buffoonery of the common people.'

Another great novelist of this period, Henry Fielding (1707-54), was the first writer to make one of his young characters a human scarecrow. Fielding is perhaps best known for his picaresque novel *Tom Jones* (1749) but he came to public attention with his parody *The History and Adventures of Joseph Andrews* (1742), in which his knowledge of country affairs is skilfully interwoven with the romance. In the second chapter of the novel he describes the formative years of his hero:

> At ten years old (by which time his education was advanced to writing and reading) he was bound an apprentice, according to the statute, to Sir Thomas Booby. Sir Thomas having an estate in his own hands, the young Andrews was at first employed in what in the country they call keeping birds. His office was to perform the part the ancients assigned to the god Priapus, which deity the moderns call by the name of Jack o' Lent; but his voice being so extremely musical, that it rather allured the birds than terrified them, he was soon transplanted from the fields into the dog-kennel, where he was placed under the huntsman, and made what the sportsmen term whipper-in.

A modern descendant of Henry Fielding, Andrew Fielding, wrote a novel in 1937 which he entitled *Scarecrow*. It was, however, a detective story in no way related to the 'man of straw' save in the unprepossessing appearance of the hero who used a mastery of unlikely disguises to trap the villain of the case.

Robert Lloyd (1733-64), who wrote the earliest complete poem to feature a scarecrow. He is also of interest because, while he was at Cambridge, he and a hell-raising friend, the satirist Charles Churchill, earned the nickname 'The

Scare-Crows' because of their constantly dishevelled appearance and wildly drunken exploits. Dissolute and impecunious, Lloyd blamed literary critics for his failure to gain fame and wealth and two years before his death condemned them in verse:

> Critics, who like scarecrows stand,
> Upon the poet's common land.
> Scarers of all winged prose,
> Mute in their praise of verse.

One writer who rarely suffered at the hands of critics was the novelist Charles Dickens (1812-70) – it was plagirists stealing his characters and plots who blighted his career. His contribution to the history of the scarecrow appears in *Nicholas Nickleby* (1838) during that famous scene at Mr Wackford Squeers' school, Dotheboys Hall, where Nicholas is introduced to the pupils: a pale, haggard and bony collection of boys looking neglected and ill-treated – ' ... half-a-dozen scarecrows, out at knees and elbows'

Less than a decade later came the first story to feature a scarecrow not just as a passing figure or as an analogy but as the central character. It was created by the American Nathaniel Hawthorne (1804-64) in his short story 'Feathertop', published in *Mosses From An Old Manse* in 1846.

Born in witch-haunted Salem, Hawthorne drew on his knowledge of rural New England customs as well as the supernatural in telling this tale of the old crone Mother Rigby who used witchcraft to create a most elegant scarecrow and give it life to take revenge on her persecutor, the local magistrate, Justice Gookin.

> The most important item of all, probably, although it made so little show, was a certain broomstick, on which Mother Rigby had taken many an airy gallop at midnight, and which now served the scarecrow by way of a spinal column, or, as the unlearned phrase it, a backbone. One of its arms was a disabled flail which used to be wielded by Goodman Rigby, before his spouse worried him out of this troublesome world; the other, if I mistake not, was composed of the pudding stick

THE SCARECROW IN LITERATURE

The Devil brings the scarecrow, Feathertop, to life in Nathaniel Hawthorne's pioneer short story written in 1846

from the woodpile. Its lungs, stomach, and other affairs of that kind were nothing better than a meal bag stuffed with straw. Thus we have made out the skeleton and entire corporation of the scarecrow, with the exception of its head; and this was admirably supplied by a somewhat withered and shrivelled pumpkin, in which Mother Rigby cut two holes for the eyes, and a slit for the mouth, leaving a bluish-coloured knob in the middle to pass for a nose. It was really quite a respectable face.

But the clothes, in this case, were to be the making of the man. So the good woman took down from a peg an ancient plum-coloured coat of London make, and with relics of embroidery on its seams, cuffs, pocket flaps, and button holes, but lamentably worn and faded, patched at the elbows, tattered at the skirts, and threadbare all over. To match the coat there was a velvet waistcoat of very ample size and formerly embroidered with foliage that had been as brightly golden as the maple leaves in October, but which had now quite vanished out of the substance of the velvet. Next came a pair of scarlet breeches, once worn by the French governor of Louisbourg, and the knees of which had touched the lower step of the throne of Louis le Grand.

Furthermore, Mother Rigby produced a pair of silk stockings and put them on the figure's legs, where they showed as unsubstantial as a dream, with the wooden reality of the two sticks making itself miserably apparent through the holes. Lastly, she put her dead husband's wig on the bare scalp of the pumpkin, and surmounted the whole with a dusty three-cornered hat, in which was stuck the longest tail feather of a rooster.

(It is this feather that gives the scarecrow his name.) With the aid of witchcraft and a magic pipe which Mother Rigby thrusts in his mouth and commands him to suck, he comes alive, to be despatched on his mission to woo and win the despised Justice's daughter. There is a clever twist to the end of the story which has been neatly described in a programme for the theatrical version of the tale called *The Scarecrow*, written in 1908 by Percy MacKaye, first staged by the Harvard Dramatic Club, transferring to New York in 1910:

'Goody Rickby, a witch of 17th Century New England, fashions a scarecrow into which she breathes life, and under the name of Lord Ravensbane, sends him to the home of Justice Merton, her former lover. Merton is forced to betroth the scarecrow to his niece, Rachel, who, believing him to be a man, falls in love with him. Her former fiancée, Richard Talbot, reveals the scarecrow's true identity, and Ravensbane, in order to ensure a happy life for Rachel, throws away the brimstone-burning pipe that gave him life, and, dignified by her love and his noble action, dies, a man.'

THE SCARECROW IN LITERATURE 75

The success of Percy MacKaye's play on Broadway led to an equally impressive film version made in 1923, entitled *Puritan Passions*. (See Chapter 4.)

In Britain, it was to be almost half a century before the first story entirely devoted to a scarecrow was written, but in the interim several notable writers made some interesting references.

George Eliot (1819-80), whose pen-name concealed the identity of Mary Ann Evans, first wrote of scarecrows in an article about farm life in the late 1850s published in the *Westminster Review* in which, driving home a point about the stubbornness of farmers to raise their livestock and crops in the face of insurmountable odds, she enquired, 'Can *you* frighten the blind with scarecrows?'

In her novel *Adam Bede* (1859) she made reference to the scarecrow using his old name of 'mawkin'. A farmer's wife, Mrs Poyser, reprimands her housemaid, Molly, for wanting to go off spinning: ' ... I hired you at Treddles' on stattis, without a bit o' character – as I say, you might be grateful to be hired in that way to a respectable place; and you knew no more o' what belongs to work when you come here than the mawkin i' the field. As poor a two-fisted thing as ever I saw, you know you was!'

Another popular Victorian novelist – though he is little remembered today – was Sir Walter Besant (1836-1901), who in 1887 published *The World Went Very Well Then*, a story of high adventure. The hero of the story, Lieutenant Jack Easterbrook, has been captured by some mysterious villains and has been stripped naked by his captor; as he lies groggily on the floor wondering what to do next, an unexpected benefactor appears with a suit of clothes:

'The things which he had to put on were so old and ragged that they would scarce hold together; and they were so dirty that no ragamuffin of the street would have picked them out of the gutter; no scarecrow in the fields ever had such clothes. They consisted of nothing more than a pair of corduroy breeches, and a dirty old knitted waistcoat, both in tatters and full of holes. Nevertheless, when Jack had them on, his courage came back to him. A man feels stronger when he has put on his clothes ... '

The year 1898 saw the publication of the first short story

A ragged character from the *Westminster Review* which published George Eliot's observations on the scarecrow

written in Britain to be wholly devoted to the scarecrow, 'An Autumn Encounter' by Kenneth Grahame (1859-1932), author of *The Wind In The Willows* (1908).

'An Autumn Encounter' vividly describes the meeting of a walker and an old scarecrow guarding a harvest of ripening corn on the Berkshire Downs. The walker first sees the scarecrow as he goes up to the Downs in the morning, and for the rest of the day his mind is ' ... haunted by that hateful speck, black on the effulgence of the slope. Did I not know he was only a scarecrow, the thing might be in a way companionable: a pleasant suggestive surmise, piquing curiosity, gilding this last weary stage with some magic of expectancy. But I passed close by him on my way out. Early as I was, he was already up and doing, eager to introduce himself. He leered after me as I swung down the road, mimicked my gait, as it seemed, in a most uncalled-for way: and when I looked back, he was blowing derisive kisses of farewell with his empty sleeves.'

When the storyteller returns at evening from his walk – during which time he has been quite unable to get the image of the scarecrow out of his mind – he finds the scarecrow somewhat altered:

> Now he is upon a new tack. Though here on the level it is still sultry and airless, an evening breeze is playing briskly along the slope where he stands, and one sleeve saws the air violently; the other is pointed stiffly heavenwards. It is plain enough, my poor friend! The sins of the world are a heavy burden and a grievous pain unto you. You have a mission, you must testify; it will go forth, in season and out of season. For man, he wakes and sleeps and sins betimes: but crows sin steadily, without any cessation. And this unhappy state of things is your own particular business. Even at this distance I seem to hear you rasping it: 'Salvation, damnation, damnation, salvation!' And the jolly earth smiles in the perfect evenglow, and the corn ripples and laughs all round you, and one young rook (only fledged this year, too!) after an excellent simulation of prostrate, heart-broken penitence, soars joyously away, to make love to his neighbour's wife. 'Salvation, damnation, damn – '
> A shifty wriggle of the road, and he is transformed once more. Flung back in an ecstasy of laughter, holding his lean sides, his whole form writhes with the chuckle and gurgle of merriment. Ho, ho! what a joke it was! How I took you all in! Even the rooks! What a joke is everything to be sure.

For a while the narrator stands lost in thought, and then at last he prepared to go on his way and put the scarecrow from his mind.

> Truly, I shall be glad to get quit of this heartless mummer. Fortunately I shall soon be past him. And now, behold! the old dog waxes amorous. Mincing, mowing, empty sleeve on hollow breast, he would fain pose as the most irresistible old hypocrite that ever paced a metropolitan kerb. 'Love, you young dogs,' he seems to croak, 'love is the one thing worth

living for! Enjoy your present, rooks and all, as I do!' Why, indeed, should he alone be insensible to the golden influence of the hour? More than one supple waist (alas! for universal masculine frailty!) has been circled by that tattered sleeve in days gone by; a throbbing heart once beat where sodden straw now fails to give a manly curve to the chest. Why should the coat survive, and not a particle of the passion that inspired it long ago?

At last I confront him, face to face: and the villain grins recognition, completely unabashed. Nay, he cocks his eye with a significant glance under the slouch of his shapeless hat, and his arm points persistently and with intelligence up the road. My good fellow, I know the way to the 'Dog and Duck' as well as you do: I was going there anyhow, without your officious interference – and the beer, as you justly remark, is unimpeachable. But was this really all you've been trying to say to me, this last half-hour? Well, well!

Kenneth Grahame's story undoubtedly pinpointed a number of universally held feelings about the scarecrow, and in a way no earlier piece of writing had done. Even today his portrait of the ambivalent figure holds good.

The dawn of the twentieth century saw the publication of the first novel with a scarecrow as a major character – *The Wonderful Wizard of Oz* by the American Lyman Frank Baum (1856-1919). This tale of little Dorothy Gale's exploits in the magical land just beyond the rainbow not only proved a landmark in juvenile fiction but also established the scarecrow as a character with tremendous potential for the imaginative writer. Give him a brain, Baum in effect said, and he can be as brave, resourceful and clever as the best human being in whose image he has been created. Sticks and stones cannot hurt his straw-filled body, and the only thing he need really fear is a lighted match ...

The story was partly inspired by Baum's childhood love of Grimms' Fairy Tales and partly by his ambition to provide his four young sons with something a little more exciting to read than the rather ponderous fiction then being marketed for children in the United States. Perhaps because of this fact, he found it impossible to get a publisher to take on his book, but nothing would shake his belief in the story, and so he

Frank Baum's world-famous scarecrow: first sketched by W.W. Denslow at the turn of the century

finally paid a small Chicago firm, George M. Hill, to market *The Wonderful Wizard of Oz* which his friend the newspaper cartoonist W.W. Denslow had copiously illustrated. His faith in the story was almost immediately justified: *The Wonderful Wizard of Oz* has been referred to by several critics as 'the first great children's book of the twentieth century'. Among its chief characters, the Scarecrow, Tin Woodman, Cowardly Lion and Dorothy, only the Scarecrow had a real-life original. He was an aged straw man dressed in a worn and faded blue work suit which sported a tattered straw hat and had stood for years in a field near Frank Baum's childhood home, Rose Lawn, near New York. 'I always remember him hanging there, all sort of shapeless,' Baum said years later. 'He never got moved. We just ploughed and sowed round him every year. He wasn't much use, but no one had the heart to move him. Then one winter he just got blown away. We never found a trace.' When asked if he thought the Scarecrow might have gone looking for a heart like the character in his book, the author would only smile enigmatically.

The Scarecrow's first meeting with Dorothy is one of the most memorable scenes Baum ever wrote:

> Dorothy leaned her chin upon her hand and gazed thoughtfully at the Scarecrow. Its head was a small sack stuffed with straw, with eyes, nose and mouth painted on it to represent a face. An old, pointed blue hat, that had belonged to some Munchkin, was perched on this head, and the rest of the figure was a blue suit of clothes, worn and faded, which had also been stuffed with straw. On the feet were some old boots with blue tops, such as every man wore in this country, and the figure was raised above the stalks of corn by means of the pole stuck up its back.
>
> While Dorothy was looking earnestly into the queer, pointed face of the Scarecrow, she was surprised to see one of the eyes slowly wink at her. She thought she must have been mistaken, at first, for none of the scarecrows in Kansas ever wink; but presently the figure nodded its head to her in a friendly way. Then she climbed down from the fence and walked up to it, while Toto ran around the pole and barked.
>
> 'Good day,' said the Scarecrow, in a rather husky voice.
> 'Do you speak?' asked the girl, in wonder.
> 'Certainly,' answered the Scarecrow; 'how do you do?'
> 'I'm pretty well, thank you,' replied Dorothy, politely; 'how do you do?'
> 'I'm not feeling well,' said the Scarecrow, with a smile, 'for

Roy Krenkel's 1965 sketch of Frank Baum's scarecrow

it is very tedious being perched up here night and day to scare away crows.'

'Can't you get down?' asked Dorothy.

'No, for this pole is stuck up my back. If you will please take away the pole I shall be greatly obliged to you.'

Dorothy reached up both arms and lifted the figure off the pole; for, being stuffed with straw, it was quite light.

'Thank you very much,' said the Scarecrow, when he had been set down on the ground. 'I feel like a new man.'

And so begins the odyssey of the Scarecrow's resolute search for a brain – as well as the enchantment of the story which is still avidly read today, a fact underlined most emphatically in an article on children's books in the *New York Times Book Review* in June 1985:

'An enormous, frenzied fuss has existed since the first Oz book appeared 85 years ago. Pinch-lipped librarians patrolling their domains in a mysterious national campaign against scarecrows and tin men; novelists and distinguished academics combing the Oz texts for echoes of Hawthorne and Stephen Crane; 26 more sequels by six writers; collectors auctioning off scraps of Ozabilia; an International Wizard of Oz Club with thousands of members; a new movie, *Return to Oz*; and, most important, I suppose, all these people, adult people, sitting around daydreaming of the times they sat around daydreaming as children, looking up from yellowed pages describing the wonderful Land of Oz.'

There can be no doubt that, while the scarecrow in *The Wonderful Wizard of Oz* earned literary fame for all of his kind, he also provided the yardstick against which all successive scarecrows have to be judged. That they should in turn have proved so interesting and varied is a credit both to their creators and also to the very special aura which the Oz scarecrow demonstrated was to be found in even the most unlikely member of his fraternity.

Of the twentieth-century British stories about scarecrows the first was by Edith King Hall (1870-1935), the daughter of a Shropshire farmer who wrote a large number of children's books, notably *The Story of the Scarecrow*, published in 1907 and illustrated in her own naïve but charming style. In a foreword to the story, she revealed that the central character was based on a scarecrow her father had made when she was a child. Here is an extract from the chapter entitled 'The Scarecrow's Secret':

> Out in the open country one breezy morning, the Traveller saw a scarecrow standing in the middle of a ploughed field. For a scarecrow he was rather well dressed, having almost a complete pair of trousers, the ragged remains of an old jacket, and on the top of his head a battered and well-ventilated bowler hat. He was tossing his arms about and beckoning as if to attract someone's attention. So the Traveller paused, waved back, and shouted, 'How fares it with you, my friend?'
> 'Fine!' replied the scarecrow. 'Fine! I scare them all right. They're all frightened of *me*. Round and round they come and I – well, I just wait for a puff of wind, then whirl my arms about and off they go. I only came last week, and had no idea it was such fun. Did you hear me sing as you came along? You didn't? Then listen:
>
>> I'm a merry Scarecrow
>>   Posted on a hill,
>> Jigging both my arms and legs
>>   To avoid a chill.
>> Once the seed is planted,
>>   The birds come down to pick;
>> But when they see me shake my fists
>>   They scatter double quick!
>> I flap my leg; I flap my sleeve,
>>   (It's all a game of make-believe)
>> But thinking I'm a living thing,
>>   They dash away on frightened wing!
>
> The scarecrow laughed gleefully, but the Traveller shook his head. 'I'm afraid,' he said, 'you have still to learn the secret.'
> '*What* secret?'
> 'Ah,' said the Traveller, 'each one must discover that for himself!'

The scarecrow does indeed try for some time to discover what 'the secret' is, and finally realizes that it is being kind to little creatures rather than scaring them away:

A charming little sketch from Edith King Hall's novel, *The Story of the Scarecrow*, published in 1907

'Yes,' said the Traveller, '*that's* the secret!' Then he chuckled and said: 'I think we ought to manage a song now. How will this do?

> Sing a song of scarecrows,
>   A pocket full of mice,
> Seeking his protection,
>   Asking his advice.
> Wind and rain and sunshine,
>   Listen to him sing,
> For since he's found the secret
>   He's happy as a King!'

This moral tale was in stark contrast to 'The Scarecrow', the title story of Gwendolyn Ranger Wormser's collection of tales first published in New York in 1918. Mrs Wormser (1868-1940) created perhaps the first truly evil scarecrow in literature. During the course of the story, she describes the influence the scarecrow has on a poor widow and her son desperately trying to wrest a living from their fields. The figure is dressed in an old military uniform that once belonged to the woman's father, and it has the uncanny habit of moving even when there is not the slightest trace of wind. It is gradually hypnotizing the young boy, Benny, as he confesses to his mother one day:

> 'S'pose – ,' he whispered. 'S'pose when it starts moving like that – s'pose some day it walks out of that corn field! Just naturally walks out here to me. What then, if it walks out?'
> 'Benny – !'
> 'That's what I'm thinking of all the time. If it takes it into its head to just naturally walk out here. What's going to stop it, if it wants to walk out after me; once it starts moving that way? What?'
> 'Benny – ! It couldn't do that! It couldn't!'
> 'Mebbe it won't. Mebbe it'll just beckon first. Mebbe it won't come after me. Not if I go when it beckons. I kind of figure it'll beckon when it wants me. I couldn't stand the other. I couldn't wait for it to come out here after me. I kind of feel it'll *beckon*. When it beckons, I'll be going.'

Despite all the widow's protestations that the scarecrow is just a scarecrow, it does indeed beckon one dark, oppressive night, and the boy is drawn away, never to be seen again ...

There was also something uncanny in Vera Menteth's story 'The Scarecrow' published in the British periodical *Pearson's Magazine* in February 1921. Miss Menteth (1890-1956), a writer of clever crime stories, pictured the scarecrow as a brooding eyewitness to a case of infidelity and murder at the farm near where he stood. She described the sentinel thus:

> It was not a pretty thing, this scarecrow of Old Man Digby's – tall and strong it stood, so for miles you might see it, black and heavy against the sky, an old coat hung about the crossed sticks, while a green feather, jaunty and long, stuck out from the rakish, flapping hat – ugly enough it was, even the horses thought that, and did a few capers before they could be made to pass it.
> But not all the protestations of Sara made any difference to Tom, there it remained down in the barley field, menacing enough, with its long, empty sleeves fluttering in the wind. An

object of fun a scarecrow might be, but there was something queer about Tom Digby's. And meantime, Sara went about her duties in the farmhouse sure it was an omen of disaster.

Just how right her premonition proves to be is revealed when her lover, Harry, suddenly goes missing. The scarecrow now moves to centre stage in the drama:

> The first drops of rain were falling as she left the house and ran down the path to where she knew Harry would be waiting. But there was no Harry and no trap, only the silence of the fields and the heavy rumble of thunder; only the mocking, muttering wind and the twisting, jagging lightning, only – oh, God, the scarecrow!
> She found herself staring at it and all the world spinning round her, saw in her terror a black crow dart with a grating, jeering caw from beneath the hat, which so jerked fell flopping to the ground: saw, as her world spun and twisted about her, that the whole vile thing was towering above her and that Harry's stripped and nearly naked body, Harry's pallid face, Harry's leaden, ash-like eyes were staring at her, fixed on her, muddy, discoloured, ghastly – showing panic – showing death.
> A farmer driving his squelching horse through the streaming rain saw, as he passed Lone Tree Farm, a woman at the foot of the scarecrow clawing, screaming at something that hung motionless and sodden from those heavy sticks; saw her and saw the battered thing that hung there, and in his terror beat his maddened horse across the Moor.

These two tales opened up a whole new range of sinister possibilities for the scarecrow in fiction: since then there has been an almost continual stream of macabre short stories about them.

The years between the two World Wars were to prove particularly fruitful where the literature of scarecrows was concerned. First there appeared a trio of novels by major writers; secondly, two highly individual fictional characters were born whose fame remains undiminished to this day. The novels were by Sir Hugh Walpole, Alfred Noyes and Clemence Dane; the characters were Dr Syn, alias 'The Scarecrow', and the lackadaisical but loveable Worzel Gummidge.

THE SCARECROW IN LITERATURE

The first of the novels was *The Golden Scarecrow* by Sir Hugh Walpole (1884-1941). Published in 1915, it was described by one reviewer as 'an excellently crafted story of the influence the chance sighting of a golden scarecrow has on one man's life – despite the fact that the mawkin is no more than an illusion'. Though Hugh Walpole was born in New Zealand, he grew up in Cornwall, and there is strong circumstantial evidence that *The Golden Scarecrow* was inspired by just such an encounter there as he describes in the course of the novel:

> They had come to a rise in the Polwint Road. To their right, running to the very foot of their path, was the moor. It stretched away, like a cloud, vague and indeterminate to the horizon. To their left a dark brown field rose in an ascending wave to a ridge that cut the sky, now crocus-coloured. The field was lit with the soft light of the setting sun. On the ridge of the field something, suspended, it seemed in mid-air, was shining like a golden fire.
> 'What's that?' said Mr Pidgen again. 'It's hanging. What the devil!'
> They stopped for a moment, then started across the field. When they had gone a little way Mr Pidgen paused again.
> 'It's like a man with a golden helmet. He's got legs, he's coming to us.'
> They walked on again. Then Hugh cried, 'Why, it's only an old Scarecrow! We might have guessed.'
> The sun, at that instant, sank behind the hills and the world was grey.
> The Scarecrow, perched on the high ridge, waved its tattered sleeves in the air. It was an old tin can that had caught the light; the can hanging over the stake that supported it in drunken fashion seemed to wink at them. The shadows came streaming up from the sea and the dark woods below in the hollow drew closer to them.
> The Scarecrow seemed to lament the departure of the light. 'Here, mind,' he said to the two of them, 'you saw me in my glory just now and don't you forget it. I may be a knight in shining armour after all. It only depends upon the point of view.'
> 'So it does,' said Mr Pidgen, taking his hat off; 'you were very fine – I shan't forget.'

Alfred Noyes' novel *The Return of the Scarecrow*, published in 1929, featured a scarecrow whose image seems to overshadow events in the lives of Sussex country folk whose existence is threatened by a combination of urban encroachment and political unease. Noyes (1880-1958), a Staffordshire-born poet who wrote such classic imaginative verses as 'The Highwayman' and 'Forty Singing Seamen', possessed a vivid knowledge of the realities of rural life which he demonstrated to considerable effect in *The Return of the Scarecrow*. The following extract describes a method of making a scarecrow which has been practised in the southernmost parts of England for generations.

Away on the downs, in a remote spot where the cultivated land spreads its last fields, Double Dick sat on a bank and turned over the collection of rags that Thorn, the shepherd, had brought up with him. Thorn drove the central stake into the ground, and lashed on to it the crosspiece which was to extend the arms of a scarecrow.

'Them arms look to you too long?' said Thorn to that other scarecrow – the ragged man on the bank.

'A bit of jut-out at the end of the sleeves won't do no harm,' said Double Dick. 'If you has no objections, Muster Thorn, this here's a better hat nor mine, and a better coat nor mine.'

'So I'd reckoned,' said Thorn, 'but felt kind of delicate-like 'bout putting it forward ... Pitch me over your own coat and hat and put these here on instead; and *you'll* look a better man, and *I'll* build a better scarecrow.'

Double Dick made the exchange with alacrity.

'Mind you,' said Thorn, as he placed the scarecrow's trousers *in situ* and stuffed them out with bracken, 'mind you, Double Dick, it's Farmer Bloxham's interests as I'm acting in. Wouldn't be honest otherwise. But worse clothes make best scarecrows. There's a smell of beer on this coat of yours as would ... well, well, find us a nice handy bit of chalk. I shall want that by'n'by.'

Thorn went on with his task, glancing from time to time at Double Dick, as an artist glances at his model. He trimmed a big swede with his knife and fixed it securely on the central pole. He whitened the front half with chalk, leaving two dark circles for the eyes, a triangle for the nose, and a crescent for the mouth. Fronds of withered fern represented the hair, and were held in place by the hat. He turned up the coat collar to make the neck more realistic. He fastened to the back of the figure the windmill arrangement that gave a continuous clack and croak in a light breeze. And at last he stood back a few yards to survey the finished work. Double Dick sat up and also looked at it with interest.

There was a moment's silence, and then Double Dick said with simple conviction:

'Gord! It's *me*!'

The third of the trio of novels from this period, *The Arrogant History of White Ben*, written by Clemence Dane (1884-1960) in 1939, is arguably the most intriguing of all, for she created a wholly engrossing plot in which White Ben, the scarecrow is brought to life, successfully rids England of a plague of crows and then returns to being a scarecrow once again – only to be torn to pieces by children.

White Ben is so named because he is dressed all in white – a white mackintosh, a vicar's long white surplice, and on his head a grey top hat. The reason for this is explained early on in the book by one character who says, 'Scarecrows must be white – crows're not afraid of black or colours.'

Interesting though this bit of country lore is, the most remarkable part of Clemence Dane's book is the scene when White Ben first turns from a scarecrow into a living creature:

> He had lived a day of brightness, exaltation and terror. He had undergone transfiguration. He had been given flesh and bones. He had been garmented with religion, diplomacy, the art of war, the art of healing; for he wore a priest's vestment, a soldier's gauntlets and civilian mackintosh, a gentleman's pleasure-hat, a surgeon's coat. His past was only a little less dim to him in the light of that transfiguration than a human being's pre-natal memories. In the past he had known darkness and light only, with heat and cold, flapping wings, the stink of mildew and crow-droppings, and the agonising whistle of the spring wind through his wooden frame. In the past he had suffered with the creatures of the field; but now men's memories were buttoned about him. The creatures of his past recognised the change and swung their censers before him in worship. Then he also was moved to worship.
>
> 'I thank thee, Lord,' he prayed, 'that I am not as other scarecrows. I have said farewell to the ditch, the right-of-way, the rustling corn. I have eyes in my head. My mouth has been opened. On my finger is a ring, a sky-blue pentacle of power. Blood reddens my breast of straw and a heart roots in me. My manikin heart has power to make a queen of England. Did not the gardener say so? Yes, and I am fit to hold a stick

in my hand, and I know how to brandish my fist. I have a name of my own. I am Ben. I am White Ben, God's Ben ... '
Then he broke off, a dizzy scarecrow, for the night-wind had taken him by the arms and was twirling him like a windmill.

He struggled furiously; but he was pegged into the soil, helpless till the wind left him. Then the weight of his free foot swung him back into position, facing the cornfield once more. Pride filled him at that.

'I return to my watch. I am faithful,' said White Ben.

The first of two scarecrow characters to appear in the inter-war years who have stood the test of time was the multi-faceted Dr Syn created by Russell Thorndike (1885-1971).

Syn was ostensibly the Vicar of Dymchurch but under the alias of 'The Scarecrow' led a band of smugglers, the Night-riders, on daring missions across Romney Marsh in the

Russell Thorndike, the creator of the famous Doctor Syn, a.k.a. 'The Scarecrow', pictured here (*left*) with George Arliss, the first man to bring the character to the screen in 1937

first years of the nineteenth century. He was also a man of formidable intellect, an excellent duellist, a skilled horseman and a friend of the Prince Regent. In a series of seven books, Thorndike pitted his hero against a variety of lawmen and villains, who pursued him relentlessly, crying their slogan, 'Death to the Scarecrow' – but invariably at his rapidly disappearing back!

The key to Dr Syn's success was his mastery of disguise and ability to discover what his enemies were up to. By day he would often take the place of a scarecrow standing eagle-eyed on Romney Marsh – and from such activities earned his nickname. Then at night he and his men would mask themselves, paint their horses with white paint and gallop through the darkness, to the terror of those who tried to stop them.

Syn proved immediately popular with readers, and Thorndike followed the first tale with six more adventures of 'The Scarecrow' as well as adapting the first book for the London Theatre in 1926 – and taking the lead role himself. In fact, *Syn* played to large audiences for almost twelve months and then graduated to the cinema screen. (See p.117.)

Of all the scarecrows in literature, Worzel Gummidge probably least needs an introduction. For half a century he has been a favourite with children as well as being a star on both radio and, latterly, television. It is not widely appreciated, however, that the irascible but loveable scarecrow from Half-acre field on Scatterbrook Farm actually first appeared on radio in the nightly programme *Children's Hour* and only after his success on the airwaves was put into print.

Worzel was created in 1935 by Barbara Euphan Todd (1903-76), who based him directly on a ragged old scarecrow that had stood in the garden of her Yorkshire home, Arksey Vicarage near Doncaster, when she was a child. She was making up poems and stories as early as eight years of age, and one of her tales, which unfortunately has not survived, was about the scarecrow which stood in the vicarage garden – though the character has no name, he was undoubtedly a forerunner of Worzel himself.

Although during her busy writing life, Barbara Euphan

The original concept of Worzel Gummidge as drawn by Elizabeth Alldridge for the first of Barbara Euphan Todd's books, *Worzel Gummidge*, published in 1936

THE SCARECROW IN LITERATURE

Todd was to produce over thirty novels for children, not to mention several plays, it was her numerous radio scripts about Worzel and his scarecrow friends, followed by the books, which made her famous. In time, there grew up a huge following for Worzel, his wife, Earthy Mangold, Scairey Gummidge, Mildew Turmut, Hannah Harrow, Aunt Sally and the rest, as well as the two children who shared their adventures, John and Susan, and the fearsome Mrs Bloomsbury-Barton. In 1955 Barbara Euphan Todd declared:

> Worzel Gummidge may well have helped to keep scarecrows alive in the country, for a great many farmers had given up using them when I was growing up. But I'm told Worzel's popularity made some of them think again!
>
> A few years ago, there was a scarecrow-making competition at the Oxford Agricultural Show and I was invited to go along as one of the judges of the entries. The other judge was Mabel Constanduros who played Worzel's wife, Earthy Mangold. Since then I have judged others at school sports and have seen a good many Worzel Gummidges and Earthy Mangolds in village fancy-dress parades.

Barbara Euphan Todd was also proud of the fact that her scarecrow earned the distinction of being mentioned in the House of Commons – and was reported in *Hansard*. 'One MP addressed another as "Nothing but a Worzel Gummidge",' she said, smiling at the memory. 'He has also been mentioned in newspapers and magazines many times, and even cropped up during a televised debate at the Oxford Union!'

Worzel was a favourite on BBC Radio for a quarter of a century. In the first broadcasts in the 1930s he was played by the rustic-voiced Hugh E. Wright; in 1945 the role was taken over by Philip Wade, and in the 1950s that much-loved broadcaster of a hundred voices Norman Shelley brought Worzel to life over the radio.

A particular feature of the radio stories were the songs that the scarecrows would sing, encouraging listeners to join in. A typical example is taken from the adventure called 'Sail Alone O' Me', broadcast on 7 November 1945, during which Saucy Nancy sang the following lines to Worzel and his friends before taking them on a boat trip:

> Ye Scairey-crows of dry-land,
> Your little fields have bounds,
> Come sail with me and you shall see,
> The sun upon his rounds.
> The sea-flowers bloom year out, year in,
> The Plough is in the sky.
> As you sail, as you sail,
> And the time goes passing by,
> And you will forget the fields you knew
> As the time goes passing by.

In this same story, Earthy Mangold also explains why scarecrows eat only raw food:

'I knew a scarecrow once as ate a potato off of the ashes of a bonfire, and she's never been the same since. Took a deep breath, she did, arter she'd swallowed and that set the potato flarin' up. You ought to have seen the smoke comin' out of her mouth – smoke and sparks and all sorts. Luckily it come on to rain, so she tipped her head back so's the water could run right down her mouth. She'd a been worse off still if she'd not got an old kettle lid fixed in the pit of her stummick. It's not all of us is as lucky as that. There's nobody can call me faddy, but I've never fancied cooked food arter that!'

One of the longest serving narrators of the stories was David Kossoff, who remembered the series with great affection all his life. He was also a talented sketch artist and drew the picture of Worzel Gummidge reproduced here together with one by Elizabeth Alldridge who illustrated the first stories when they were published in 1936. These pictures closely resemble Barbara Euphan Todd's own idea of Worzel – an impression which has been largely altered by Jon Pertwee's interpretation of the character in the recent television serial.

Barbara Euphan Todd's first book, *Worzel Gummidge*, gives a clear description of Worzel: 'The children could see that the scarecrow was dressed in an old black coat and long trousers, and that its hat was tilted on to the back of its head. Its arms were stuck straight out from its shoulders. Susan saw that the scarecrow had a most friendly and pleasant face. It was cut out of a turnip, and one or two green leaves stuck out from under his black bowler hat. She looked more closely, and

Broadcaster David Kossoff's sketch of Worzel Gummidge

saw that the scarecrow hadn't got a hand. The round, polished end of a broom-handle showed beyond his ragged cuff.'

When Worzel speaks, he describes himself not as a scarecrow but as a 'stand still': 'I am a stand-still, that's what I am,' he says. 'I've been standing still, rain and fine, day in and day out, roots down and roots up.'

His creator describes the scarecrow as 'a nice sort of betwixt and between person, not quite grown up though he seemed as old as the fields, and yet not quite a child either, though in some ways he seemed as young as they were'.

Worzel also explains that he chose his name himself, even though he had a grandfather named Bogle. When it is pointed out by Susan and John that Worzel is not a very pretty name, he agrees: 'No – it's as ugly as I am!'

Gummidge as portrayed in Southern Television's production starring Jon Pertwee

And when asked how old he is, he replies: 'All manner of ages! My face is one age, and my feet are another, and my arms are the oldest of the lot. That's the way it is with scarecrows – and it's a good way, too. I get a lot of birthdays, you see, one for my face and another for my middle and another for my hands, and so on!'

Barbara Euphan Todd's eight books about Worzel Gummidge have continued to delight readers through half a century, and following the television series three more new collections of stories by the scriptwriters of the series, Keith Waterhouse and Willis Hall, have been published by Puffin Books. Interestingly, the first of Barbara Euphan Todd's books was used to launch this now famous paperback imprint for children in 1941, and in 1981 a special facsimile edition of *Worzel Gummidge* was released to mark its fortieth anniversary.

Since the advent of Worzel Gummidge, the scarecrow has featured in a number of works of fiction, almost exclusively from British and American writers.

The British poet and novelist Walter de la Mare (1873-1956) was something of a champion of the scarecrow in much the same way as Barbara Euphan Todd. He too was dismayed to see that they had disappeared from far too many farmers' fields, and in the 1930s and forties he wrote several poems and stories which underlined their effectiveness.

For instance, in one short story, 'Crewe' (1932), de la Mare described a scarecrow which frightened both crows and men. 'There was something in the appearance of the thing,' he wrote, 'something in the way it bore itself up, so to speak, with its arms thrown up at the sky and its empty face, which wasn't what you'd expect of mere sticks and rags.'

The tale concerns the ghost of a dead man who returns and takes possession of the scarecrow in order to gain his revenge on the rival who has deprived him of his inheritance. At the climax, the narrator observes nervously: 'We know as how dead men tell no tales. Let alone scarecrows, then.'

In a second story, 'The Scarecrow or Hodmadod' (1945), de la Mare describes a man who, as a boy, sees a fairy hovering near a scarecrow known as Old Joe. When, as an adult, the man buys the scarecrow and tries to repeat the

Evocative illustration by Irene Hawkins for Walter de la Mare's story, *The Scarecrow* (1945)

experience, nothing happens because he no longer believes in such things. It is a memorable story, made all the more so by this ringing description of the scarecrow:

'Then, as now, Old Joe was the scaringest of scaring scarecrows I have ever set eyes on. But, like the primrose in the poem, he was nothing more. No, it wasn't Old Joe himself who was the fairy, no more than the house behind us *is* you and me. Old Joe was merely one of this particular fairy's rendyvouses, as the old word goes. He was where she was.' (Irene Hawkins' striking illustration for this story is reproduced here.)

De la Mare also produced one of the very few poems written from the scarecrow's point of view, which at the same time summarized his own convictions:

> All winter through I bow my head
> Beneath the driving rain;
> The North wind powders me with snow
> And blows me black again;
> At midnight 'neath the maze of stars
> I flame with glittering rime,
> And stand, above the stubble, stiff
> As mail at morning prime.
> But when that child called Spring, and all
> His host of children, come,
> Scattering their buds and dew upon
> These acres of my home,
> Some rapture in my rags awakes;
> I lift void eyes and scan
> The skies for crows, those ravening foes,
> Of my strange master, Man.
> I watch him striding lank behind
> His clashing team, and know
> Soon will the wheat swish body high
> Where once lay sterile snow;
> Soon shall I gaze across a sea
> Of sun-begotten grain
> Which my unflinching watch hath sealed
> For harvest once again.

In America, the scarecrow has of late featured in both grim and humorous stories. A little masterpiece is 'The Crow and the Scarecrow' (1956) by the humourist James Thurber, a life-long admirer of *The Wizard of Oz*. Thurber (1894-1961) had an acute eye for the foibles of American life and in his little fable describes what happens to a farmer who, having unsuccessfully tried to drive off an armada of crows with a scarecrow, dresses himself up as one and, armed with a double-barrelled shotgun, stands in a field to await their return. The climax to Thurber's story reads thus:

> Dawn broke that morning with a sound like a thousand tin pans falling. This was the rebel yell of the crows coming down on field and garden like Jeb Stuart's cavalry. Now one of the young crows who had been out all night, drinking corn instead of eating it, suddenly went into a tailspin, plunged into a bucket of red paint that was standing near the barn, and burst into flames.
>
> The farmer was just about to blaze away at the squadron of crows with both barrels when the one that was on fire headed straight for him. The sight of a red crow, dripping what seemed to be blood, and flaring like a Halloween torch, gave the living scarecrow such a shock that he dropped dead in one beat less than the tick of a watch.
>
> The next Sunday the parson preached a disconsolate sermon, denouncing drink, carryings on, adult delinquency, front page marriages, golf on Sunday, adultery, careless handling of firearms, and cruelty to our feathered friends. After the sermon, the dead farmer's wife explained to the preacher what had really happened, but he only shook his head and murmured skeptically. 'Confused indeed would be the time in which the crow scares the scarecrow and becomes the scarescarecrow.'
>
> Moral: All men kill the thing they hate, too, unless, of course, it kills them first!

Scarecrows involved in deadly situations are also to be found in American short stories such as A.E. Martin's 'The Scarecrow Murders' published in *Ellery Queen's Mystery Magazine* in April 1948, and Paul Jones' brutal tale of a murderer brought to justice in 'Scarecrow' (1966) which earned a place in the prestigious collection *Famous Short Stories* edited by Frank C. Platt.

A popular American crime novel in 1938 was Frederic Arnold Kummer's *The Scarecrow Murders* which was prefaced with these intriguing remarks:

> The scarecrow in Anthony Morrison's cornfield was a familiar figure to Sam Hopper, for he passed the field almost weekly on his way to market. On this bright November morning, however, he could not help noticing that the ragged creature looked different ... horribly different. Instead of its

A number of country magazines have published pictures and poems about the scarecrow – here is a typical cover illustration from *The Countryman*, Spring 1965

customary jauntiness, it sagged listlessly against the supporting crossbar, and as he looked more closely, Mr Hopper could see that the imaginary face beneath the battered hat-brim had suddenly become a real one, a grim and very shocking real one! What was more shocking still, three black-winged buzzards were soaring down in slow but very businesslike circles. How Anthony Morrison's scarecrow came to have such a grisly understudy is the nucleus of this swift, exciting story ...

Deadly scarecrows have likewise cropped up in some notable British stories, pre-eminently 'Jeremy in the Wind' (1949) by Nigel Kneale, the creator of the famous Quatermass stories and films; 'Mrs Anstey's Scarecrow' (1968) by publisher and author W.H. Carr and George Mackay Brown's dramatic tale set in the Orkney Islands of Scotland, 'Mister Scarecrow' (1969), which contains this evocative passage:

'At sunset a crow came and sat on the derelict shoulder of Eric Leyland's scarecrow. A thrush sang out of one of the ruined coat pockets next morning. "Well," said Eric to the scarecrow, "we've done our best. It's up to God now ... " There the scarecrow stood, a drunken dandy, tilted a little to the right, his arms blossoming with birds, rooted in the black earth. Presently a flush of braid came over the field; and soon after that the scarecrow was standing in a first green pool of corn. 'And the birds wheeled and dug and disputed and sang about him all through the deepening summer.'

The most recent story to be published in Britain using the scarecrow image became involved in a curious controversy. On the one hand Robert Westall's novel for young readers, *The Scarecrows* (1982) was banned from many school libraries for being 'sexually explicit' – it describes the impressions and feelings of a prep-school boy who witnesses from a cupboard peephole the sexual advances of his stepfather to his mother; on the other hand, it was awarded the Carnegie Medal as the most outstanding children's book of the year. Reviewers of children's books found themselves in a quandary about the work – perhaps not surprisingly. Said the *Daily Mail*: '*The Scarecrows* is a brilliant, disturbing novel ... I would not, however, want my son to read it.' The *New Statesman*: 'The writer makes a point of putting into his novel everything that children's authors used to be obliged to leave out: swearing, aggression, genuine ill feeling, sex, the lot.' And from the other side of the world, the *New Zealand Times* declared: '*The Scarecrows* is a nasty little tale, well told ... just the thing for evil little minds to tuck into during the long school holidays.'

It was perhaps rather appropriate that Robert Westall's book should have been issued in paperback by Puffin – demonstrating at a stroke how far the scarecrow in fiction had progressed from that very first book to appear on their list, *Worzel Gummidge*.

4 The Straw Man on the Screen

'You never saw such a scarecrow as he makes him.'

ANDREW MARVELL

The credit for first bringing the scarecrow to the cinema screen belongs to one of the pioneers of film-making, the French wizard Charles Pathé (1863-1957) whose name is probably more famous today than any of his individual productions, having been kept alive through the long-running weekly newsreel 'Pathé News' (the first of its kind in the world) and the 'Pathé Colour' process which he developed.

By 1909 Pathé was the world's premier film producer, forever searching for new topics. That year he made the first of what proved to be a line of pictures featuring scarecrows. Although there is no copy still in existence of this pioneer picture (called, simply, *The Scarecrow*) a review in the cinema trade magazine *The Bioscope* of 21 October 1909 indicates that it was 610 feet long, filmed in black and white and, naturally, silent; it was shot in France, in the fields of Vincennes.

The review also gives the plot of the story. A farmer, seeing that his scarecrow is ineffectual against the birds in his orchard, takes its place and, so convincing is he that his own daughter does not recognize him when she dallies in the orchard with her lover. Recognizing the man as a scoundrel, the farmer throws off his disguise to intervene – and the story ends happily.

It seems highly likely that *The Scarecrow* was a success with audiences, for other film-makers were soon using similar ideas to fill the cinemas.

A year later, in October 1910, the Danish company

Half-man, half-scarecrow: Patrick McGoohan in the title role of *Doctor Syn, Alias The Scarecrow* made in 1963

Nordisk put out a silent drama identically entitled *The Scarecrow*. Somewhat longer than the Pathé picture (715 feet), this film has also been lost. Its story tells of a criminal's ruse after robbing a country farm – he disguises himself as a scarecrow and hides in a field of corn until the hue and cry has died down. However, a smart detective, suspecting what his quarry has done, catches him by the simple expedient of waiting until a bird settles on the thief's shoulder and causes him to move.

Hot on the heels of the Danish production came a British film which carried the title of *The Scarecrow*, made in 1911, at Walton-on-Thames, by Cecil Hepworth, one of the pioneer film-makers in Britain. At 350 feet long, was only half the length of its predecessors. A synopsis in a Hepwix catalogue for the month of September 1911, when it was released, refers to it as 'a comedy describing the adventures of a gentleman who is unfortunately forced to represent a scarecrow'.

Cecil Hepworth the Yorkshire-born film-maker and creator of the short comedy *The Scarecrow* in 1911

Twelve months passed and cinema audiences were offered yet *another* picture called *The Scarecrow*. This latest film, from Cines, was from Italy and at 980 feet was both longer and more ambitious than the trio which had gone before. Although production and cast details are unknown, a precis of the silent film can be found in *The Bioscope* of 1 August 1912. Briefly, the story tells how a farmer, who has sold his cattle at the market, makes the homeward journey with a parcel of notes in his pocket-book and is waylaid by robbers. They stow the money in the pocket of a coat worn by a scarecrow in one of the fields, so a police search of them reveals nothing, and they are allowed to go. On his way home, wet and dispirited, the farmer meets a friend who gives him the scarecrow's coat to protect him from the cold. Putting his hand in the pocket, he discovers his missing pocket-book. When he tells the police his story, guessing that the thieves will return for their booty, a sergeant makes plans.

The ruffians cautiously approach the scarecrow, but as they go to open the coat, the figure suddenly throws its arms tightly round one of them – the sergeant has taken the place of the dummy! – and the other rogue is captured by the officers.

The similarities between this plot and that of the earlier popular Pathé picture are self-evident, and it stands as an early example of the kind of plagiarism to which film companies were prone. None the less, the picture was successful in Italy and was also shown in quite a number of British cinemas in 1912.

As if no one was able to think of an alternative title, a fifth picture named *The Scarecrow* appeared in April 1913. The makers this time were a small French company named Nizza, though the distribution of the 455-foot silent film was arranged by none other than Pathé, who clearly had no objections to the similarity with their own pioneer picture.

According to the Pathé catalogue of April 1913, the film was about 'a scarecrow who meets with many surprising adventures and is responsible for some very comical situations'. It seems a little sweeping to talk of 'many adventures' in a film that lasted less than five minutes, but the idea of a scarecrow starring as a character in his own right was certainly unusual – though not new, for by that time Frank Baum's scarecrow in the story of *The Wonderful Wizard of Oz* had made his screen debut. It is just possible that the Nizza film might have been inspired by the first Oz picture, made in 1910, but no print has survived for comparison.

The transfer of Frank Baum's story to the screen is much better documented.

Entrepreneurs in the world of entertainment have always been quick to seize on successful books for adaptation, and *The Wonderful Wizard of Oz* proved no exception. Soon after the book's publication, Baum was approached by an American theatrical producer, Fred Hamlin, and commissioned to turn the book into a stage musical, with Paul Tietjens, a Chicago composer, providing the music. This adaptation required Dorothy to become a teenager and also emphasized the parts of the Scarecrow and the Tin

Fred Stone who, with his partner, David Montgomery, first brought to life Frank Baum's scarecrow in the 1903 stage version of *The Wizard of Oz*

Woodman. Vivacious Anna Laughlin was cast as Dorothy, and the long-established comedy team of Fred Stone and David Montgomery played the Scarecrow and his metal friend.

The musical – lavish by any standards, with huge, colourful sets and a large cast – opened in Chicago in June 1902 to press and public acclaim. In January 1903 it transferred to the Majestic Theatre in New York and there enjoyed a record-breaking run of 293 performances, making Broadway stars of Stone and Montgomery.

The performance of Fred Stone (1873-1959) as the scarecrow set a standard for all those who were later to play the part on stage and screen, but little evidence beyond some photographs and reviews remains of his role. Years later, when he was making films as well as occasionally appearing in the theatre, he was to recall with great pride how he became the first actor to play the scarecrow in *The Wizard of Oz*: 'I just read the book over and over again and tried to make myself as much like the Scarecrow as I could – wobbly, awkward, but loveable' he said when interviewed in 1935. 'I didn't believe it was possible to do any better than model myself on Frank Baum's own description.'

Fred Stone knew this description so well he could recite it word for word: 'The Scarecrow's body was only a suit of clothes filled with straw. The coat was buttoned tight to keep the packed straw from falling out and a rope was tied around the waist to hold it in shape and prevent the straw from sagging down. The Scarecrow's head was a gunnysack filled with bran, on which the eyes, nose and mouth had been painted. His hands were white cotton gloves stuffed with fine straw. But even when carefully stuffed and patted into shape, the straw man was awkward in his movements and decidedly wobbly on his feet.'

After *The Wizard of Oz* had finished its run on Broadway, the musical toured America for the next decade, making Frank Baum even more aware of the public's delight at his story. He decided to capitalize on the triumph himself by touring and lecturing about Oz to paying audiences. It would also enable him to promote his books.

With this in mind, Baum commissioned the resourceful Selig Polyscope Company of Chicago to make what he called a 'Fairylogue' about the Land of Oz, using the stories of the three Oz books already published – *The Wonderful Wizard of Oz*, *Dorothy and the Scarecrow of Oz* and *The Land of Oz* – and providing a series of hand-tinted scenes complete with trick effects to transport viewers into the author's wonderland. Baum himself would introduce the film to his audiences and then step to one side of the stage to narrate the story which followed. The two-hour show complete with orchestral accompaniment provided by the Theodore Thomas Orchestra opened in Chicago in October 1908 but, because of the cost of creating the films, transporting the equipment to show them, and hiring musicians, Baum could not make the ends of his enterprising venture meet and the 'Travelogue' closed in New York that same Christmas.

This was not to write *finis* on Frank Baum's idea, however. The Selig Company decided that the film they had created might well become the basis of three short, one-reel movies, each using Frank Baum's original book titles. To this end they put Otis Turner, an already skilled director and scriptwriter, to work on the project, with the brief to create three 1,000-foot silents from the existing material. Playing the part of

William Selig's 'Fairylogue' about the world of Oz was to lead to the movie *His Majesty, The Scarecrow of Oz* made in 1914

Dorothy was the impish Bebe Daniels, who soon after became one of the major stars of American silent films and later a popular entertainer in Britain with her husband, Ben Lyon. The Scarecrow was played with considerable gusto by Hobart Bosworth (1867-1943).

The first of the trio, *The Wizard of Oz*, was released in March 1910, but neither this film nor its two successors (released in April 1910 and May 1911) proved a great box-office success. In fact, they were to prove the forerunners of several further unsuccessful attempts to bring the world of Oz to the screen before the classic tale achieved the acclaim it and its characters deserved.

In 1913 Baum agreed to take part in establishing a company which would adapt his books for the screen. Appropriately the new organization called itself 'The Oz Film Manufacturing Company', declaring on its letterheads its aim of making 'Special Features in Fairy Extravaganzas' – with Baum as President, and the composer Louis Gottschalk as Vice-President. These two would script and score the Oz films while the other partners raised the finance to create a studio on a seven-acre site on Santa Monica Boulevard. An enclosed stage was built – at the time one of the largest in the US, complete with an underground tunnel and huge water tank for special sequences.

The first story Baum wrote was *The Patchwork Girl of Oz*, based on his then current book in the series, and this went into production in July 1914 with a score by Gottschalk and directed by John Farrell MacDonald. Starring as Scraps, the 'Patchwork Girl' brought to life by magic, was a French acrobat called Pierre Couderc, who liked to refer to himself as 'The Marvellous Couderc'.

Dorothy did not appear in this story, but there was a prominent role for the Scarecrow, who falls in love with the Patchwork Girl. The part in the film was played by Herbert Glennon (1895-1967), who in later years became a director of photography and was behind the camera on *The Ten Commandments* (1923), and *Stagecoach* (1939).

Baum and his associates in the Oz Film Manufacturing Company put considerable effort into making and promoting their first picture, but its reception at the box office was, to their surprise and dismay, luke-warm. The public, who had read the Oz books in their hundreds of thousands, just did not turn up to see them on the screen. One reason given for this, according to historian Murray Glass, was that, 'Baum failed to take into account the difference in media between the book source and the requirements of the screen'; another explanation, offered by the author's eldest son, Frank junior, was that adult cinema-goers objected to having 'kid movies' shown in the theatres. Some of them apparently, even demanded their money back!

However, Frank Baum was not deterred by this setback to his grand plans, and decided to take over the directing of the sequel himself with a completely new story entitled *His Majesty, the Scarecrow of Oz*, to which Louis Gottschalk again contributed the score. Firmly convinced by all the letters he received from readers that the Scarecrow was the favourite character in his books, Baum thrust him to the forefront of the five-reel tale, in which Dorothy and the Tin Woodman also returned.

A talent hunt was started to find the right actor to play the role of the Scarecrow, and finally the part went to an actor who had had a small part in the earlier film – the versatile Frank Moore (1888-1960), who claimed to have played a scarecrow in his earlier days as a vaudeville actor. Certainly, he was loose-limbed and energetic, with a background in short comedy films, and had evidently seen the various interpretations his predecessors had made of the part. Equipped with this knowledge, Moore played the brave-hearted Scarecrow who leads a successful attack against the despotic King Krewl and is rewarded for his triumph by being made the King of Oz. Moore was undoubtedly at his best in the film during the moments of comedy, and with the aid of concealed wires played a wonderful scene when he was snatched from off a pole in the beak of a huge crow.

Although this film was later to inspire a book, *The Scarecrow of Oz*, published in 1915, distributors were reluctant to take it after the failure of *The Patchwork Girl*. Indeed, it obtained distribution only when taken over by a small company named Alliance Films, who insisted on a title change to *The New Wizard of Oz*, hoping that this might cause it to be associated in the public's mind with the successful stage musical.

The top Hollywood comedian, Larry Semon, whose 1925 version of *The Wizard of Oz* was a failure at the box office

The failure of this second Oz picture just about broke Frank Baum's heart, and though the Oz Film Manufacturing Company tried to recoup some of their losses with a modern drama called *The Last Egyptian*, which Baum also wrote, the company was forced to go out of business in the autumn of 1915.

Baum died in 1919, just six years before the next attempt was made to bring Oz to the screen. In the light of what happened, that might be said to have been a merciful release.

The version of *The Wizard of Oz* made in 1925 was very much the personal object of Larry Semon (1889-1928), at that time one of the most popular and highly paid comedians in Hollywood, a man able to draw audiences every bit as large as those of Chaplin, Lloyd and Keaton. He made a speciality of playing white-faced, dumb characters – which, in all probability, is what superficially attracted him to the part of the Scarecrow in *The Wizard of Oz*. However, his playing of the part in this mocking style contributed to the picture's failure, for, as historian Allen Eyles has written, 'Semon's subsequent treatment probably offended anyone who loved Baum's work.'

Semon not only wrote the script for his *Wizard of Oz* but also directed the picture (though he did employ Frank Baum's eldest son as a script consultant) and starred his wife, Dorothy Dwan, as Dorothy. Much of the original story in Oz was removed from the film to be replaced by scenes of slapstick comedy with Semon alternately playing a dumb farmhand and an even dumber scarecrow.

An interesting feature of the film was the appearance of a certain Oliver N. Hardy as another farmhand who at one point masqueraded as the Tin Woodman. This same Oliver Hardy was a few years later to team up with Stan Laurel to form the most famous comedy team in film history.

Although the film was generally well reviewed, ' ... it found little favour with audiences,' according to Murray Glass, 'and was soon withdrawn.' This in spite of such glowing praise as appeared in *Photoplay Magazine* for June 1925: 'If you don't take the children to see this they'll never forgive you. Nothing quite so funny as Larry Semon in the role of the Scarecrow has happened in a long time.... All the characters that Montgomery and Stone made famous are there, including the

Wizard and the Tin Woodman played by Charlie Murray and Oliver Hardy, with a lot of clever new business to add to the merriment.'

In 1920 Semon's rival Buster Keaton (1895-1966) had made what is now looked upon as the first classic scarecrow picture – a film once again called *The Scarecrow*, of which the film historian Leslie Halliwell wrote recently, 'Keaton's unique comic sense and inventive genius fill this two-reeler with sublime gags.'

The story, written by Keaton himself, assisted by Eddie Cline, drew on the traditions of the American scarecrow as a part of the rural scene. Keaton played a scarecrow who comes alive and, as so often in his pictures, falls foul of machinery. His co-stars were Sybil Seely and Joe Roberts.

Rudi Blesh, in his 1966 biography of the star, commented: '*The Scarecrow* ... is a bit of a fantasy, a kind of sublimation or distillation of slapstick. Buster plays an animated scarecrow who might have come from *The Wizard of Oz*. He is a hermit – or, if you choose, an outcast – who lives in a shack full of hilarious homemade mechanical devices. It is an unearthly little comedy.... It is the poetry of memory....'

Three years later the first feature-length movie about a scarecrow, *Puritan Passions*, also made in America took its place alongside Keaton's production as an acknowledged classic. It was based on 'Feathertop' by Nathaniel Hawthorne and had come to the screen via Percy Mackaye's 1908 stage adaptation entitled *The Scarecrow* (p.74).

Puritan Passions was a 1½ hour silent feature made by Frank Tuttle (1892-1963), a former film critic and publicity writer who had entered films in the early twenties as a screenwriter and quickly turned to directing. Not only did he script the picture: he also raised the finance, directed the filming and then organized its distribution through Film-Guild Hodkinson. Its ultimate triumph was, therefore, very much his.

In the role of the scarecrow, Tuttle cast Glenn Hunter (1892-1969), a tall and rather reserved Californian stage actor, with Osgood Perkins as Dr Nicholas, the man who brings him alive, and Mary Astor as the girl with whom he falls in love. (For the plot, see p.74). The tautly directed and atmospheric picture which Tuttle produced was well received

The great Buster Keaton playing a man of straw who is brought to life in *The Scarecrow* which he wrote and directed in 1920

by the critics, who saw it as 'a commendable attempt to render fantasy in American terms' and 'a combination of the Faust and Frankenstein themes'.

Puritan Passions has had many admirers over the years, foremost among them Carlos Clarens, author of *The History of the Horror Film*, who wrote in 1967: 'Deprived of sound and dialogue, director Frank Tuttle retained a good part of the play's poetic quality by making the picture strikingly visual and borrowing the barest of influence (like a blacksmith shop set) from German films. There were scenes of supernatural horror, as when the weird, misshapen creatures of the netherworld meet for the Witches' Sabbath or the episode of the Mirror of Truth, borrowed from

Goethe's *Faust*, where sinners see themselves as they really are.'

Another admirer of the picture was television producer Lewis Freedman who in January 1972 made the final transition of Hawthorne's story when he presented a spectacular two-hour television version of *The Scarecrow* in sound and colour for US viewers. ('Feathertop' was also broadcast as a radio play by the BBC in 1942.)

The production, which appeared under the banner of the 'Hollywood Television Theatre' series, was a faithful presentation of Percy MacKaye's play, meticulously directed by Boris Sagal, and starred Gene Wilder, an actor who has made a speciality of jittery and vulnerable characters. For his performance in 'The Scarecrow', Wilder found himself put forward for a television award in a laudatory review of the production by *The Hollywood Reporter* of 12 January 1972.

'In this two-hour drama,' the paper's TV critic, Sue

A scene from *Puritan Passions* with Maude Hill and Osgood Perkins turning the man of straw into a human being

Cameron, said, 'Gene Wilder displayed such immense acting talent that no less than an Emmy would be good enough for him.' He played a scarecrow (son of witch, Nina Foch) who was turned into Lord Ravensbane.

'Wilder's brilliance was first apparent in the scene where he came to life and started to talk and walk. Later, he had warm, beautiful scenes while he was wooing Miss Blythe Danner, but in the end he found he couldn't have her because he was really just a scarecrow and not a man. He gave a moving speech about wanting to be a man and got his wish, but as a man he died in her arms. Wilder has expressive eyes, and an attitude as the unfortunate Lord that is remarkable. His performance was a perfectly stated *tour de force*.'

The newspaper had praise for other members of the cast, too, as well as for the multi-faceted storyline. It was a tribute that would surely have delighted Nathaniel Hawthorne himself had he still been alive to see yet another triumph of his redoubtable scarecrow, Feathertop.

Another famous character who has also been brought to the screen several times made his debut in a full-length feature film a decade after Feathertop. This was Russell Thorndike's nineteenth-century adventurer Dr Syn, alias 'The Scarecrow'. The Doctor, however, appeared with the benefits of sound and location shooting at the actual site of the story. In 1937 Gaumont British brought their considerable resources, not to mention two of their most talented stars, into making the film *Dr Syn*.

Cast as the man who is a motionless 'man of straw' at one moment and a charming 'man of the cloth' at the next, was George Arliss (1868-1946), considered by many to be one of the most individual not to say idiosyncratic stars of the 1930s. His polished performance was supported by the young actress Margaret Lockwood, as his daughter, and the chubby comic Graham Moffatt, as the potboy at the local inn. Moffatt, who co-starred with Will Hay in many of his famous comedies, also doubled as a look-out for the Doctor and his men – and his scene struggling to wrap straw around himself in order to become a scarecrow look-out was undoubtedly a highlight of the picture.

There was talk for a time of a sequel, but Arliss's wife suddenly and tragically lost her sight, and he promptly retired

The mysterious scarecrow look-out played by Gordon Rollings in the 1962 version of Russell Thorndike's story re-entitled, *Captain Clegg*

from the screen to look after her.

It was to be twenty-five years before *The Scarecrow* reappeared, this time played by Peter Cushing for the horror movie specialists Hammer Films. The company's reputation for filling their productions with blood and gore was well justified where this film was concerned, and it earned some fairly savage reviews. *The Daily Worker*, for instance, called it 'cheap and nasty', while Penelope Gilliatt of the *Observer* said the picture contained 'some of Hammer's most sickening make-up effects and a vile scene in which a maimed mute is made to sing'.

It was certainly true that the scriptwriter, John Elder, had taken considerable liberties with Thorndike's original story, but at least the director, Peter Graham Scott, changed the character's name to Dr Blyss and called the picture *Captain Clegg*. (In America it was known as *Night Creatures*.)

Much of the action of the film was centred around the

activities of Dr Blyss and his followers when they rode out at night as the dreaded 'Marsh Phantoms', but there were several scenes featuring scarecrow look-outs, one of whom was appropriately named Wurzel and provided some excellent comic moments. The role was memorably played by Gordon Rollings, a gangling character actor with a thin, mournful face.

By a curious twist of fate, another version of the same story, entitled *Dr Syn, Alias The Scarecrow*, was being made at much the same time by the Walt Disney Organization, though it was not released until 1963, with Patrick McGoohan in the title role. It was based on a story entitled 'Christopher Syn' by Russell Thorndike and William Buchanan, and was screened as an all-action drama, with the Scarecrow engaged in a battle of wits and weaponry against the tyrannical General Pugh, instructed by King George III to root out the Kent coast smugglers. As in the previous films, Dr Syn manages to preserve the secret of his alter ego, and the closing scenes were again carefully arranged so that a sequel was possible. Indeed, the film was later shown on American television in three parts, under the title *The Scarecrow of Romney Marsh*, and its seems highly probable that these were intended as a pilot for a full-blown series if the ratings had been high enough.

One novel element of this third version of Thorndike's story is 'The Scarecrow's Song', a memorable little number composed by Terry Gilkyson.

Music was to prove one of the key elements in what is now regarded as the most famous of all scarecrow pictures, MGM's classic 1939 version of *The Wizard of Oz*. The failures of the earlier versions of Frank Baum's novel were at last to be put to one side by the triumphant Judy Garland film – though the initial reaction to the film (the first in colour, after its opening sequence set in Kansas shot in black and white) were little short of catastrophic.

When the picture was released in August 1939, just before the outbreak of World War II, the American critic Otis Ferguson of *The New Republic* thought it weighed 'like a fruitcake soaking wet', while *Time* magazine considered it ' ... collapses like a scarecrow in a cloudburst', and *The New Yorker*'s Russel Maloney declared even more brutally, 'The

Patrick McGoohan who gave the best interpretation of Russell Thorndike's hero in *Doctor Syn, Alias The Scarecrow* in 1963

Wizard of Oz displays no trace of imagination, good taste or ingenuity. A stinkeroo.'

These verdicts did nothing but harm the picture at the box office and it was to be twenty years before MGM recouped the $2½ million it had cost to make the picture. In fact, it was not until *The Wizard of Oz* was shown on American

Ray Bolger who played the scarecrow so brilliantly in the 1939 MGM film version of *The Wizard of Oz*

television in 1956 that its true status was appreciated – and since that date not a year has passed without its being shown again on the small screen (usually at Christmas) as well as having occasional re-releases in the cinema. This transformation in the fortunes of the film was a confirmation of the faith of all those involved in making it, perhaps few more so than Ray Bolger who created the classic portrayal of a scarecrow on the screen.

The film rights in the Frank Baum books had changed hands several times since Larry Semon's ill-fated comedy version in 1925, and when in 1937 Louis B. Mayer secured them for MGM in competition with Twentieth Century Fox (who saw the story as an ideal vehicle for their child star, Shirley Temple), he put the project in the hands of the mercurial producer Mervyn Le Roy.

Le Roy had for some time been keen to film *The Wizard of Oz*, but work on the project was to undermine his enthusiasm, for it was to take ten script-writers, four directors and six months of filming (as well as over-running budget by nearly $1 million) to bring the story to the screen.

Sixteen-year-old Judy Garland was just one of several young singer-actresses considered for the part of Dorothy. The very popular Deanna Durbin, for example, was an early favourite, but the studio chiefs decided that the size of her breasts precluded her ever looking like a young girl. (Even Judy Garland had to wear a corset while filming.) This said, the picture turned Judy Garland into a star, won her a special Academy Award and provided her with a song, 'Over The Rainbow', with which her name was to be forever associated.

Supporting Judy Garland were three veterans of the worlds of American burlesque and vaudeville, Bert Lahr playing the Cowardly Lion, Jack Haley as the Tin Woodman and Ray Bolger as the Scarecrow. Like Judy Garland, Ray Bolger had not been first choice for his part. The actor earmarked for the role had been song-and-dance man Buddy Ebsen, a Broadway musical star. But fate was to decree otherwise, and Bolger got his earnest wish to play the Scarecrow. His recollections offer a fascinating insight into the background of the film.

He was actually the highest paid of the stars who appeared in *The Wizard of Oz*, earning $3,000 a week against Judy Garland's $500, but it was not money that attracted him to either the film or the role:

'I knew that I was taking part in a strange adventure,' he was to recall. 'Everything had to be invented for the picture – the effects, the sound, the Technicolor. It was all new. But when the reviews came out it was a terrific disappointment.

The picture got terrible notices. It was only when *The Wizard of Oz* came into the home with television that it redeemed itself. Then it was no longer a picture – it was an institution.'

This 'institution' might very well have featured him in a quite different role, for he was initially called into Mervyn LeRoy's office in March 1938 and told he was to play the Tin Woodman.

'It's not my cup of tea,' he protested. 'I'm not a tin performer. I'm fluid.'

But his appeal fell on deaf ears, and soon afterwards Buddy Ebsen not only had costume fittings as the Scarecrow but also began to rehearse the dance routines.

Still Bolger would not give up. 'You see I had my heart set on playing the Scarecrow,' he said years later. 'Fred Stone, who played the part in the original 1902 play, was a kind of idol of mine. When I was 15 or 16 I saw him in *Jack O'Lantern* at a theatre in Boston. All I remember now is that I saw this man save a girl from a fate worse than death. He bounded on a trampoline out of a haystack looking just like a scarecrow, put his hand on his head, and said, "Just in time!" I've never forgotten it. That moment opened up a whole new world for me.'

So Bolger persisted in his appeal to Mervyn LeRoy and MGM.

'I really fought for that part. I was signed to MGM for seven years at the time and though I was in the second year of my contract I hadn't done anything. I didn't want to play the Tin Man because that involved stiff dancing and movements of that sort which didn't interest me. I like freedom of movement, I'm that kind of actor.'

'Also, the Scarecrow was my favourite part in the Oz books, so I was determined that no one else was going to get that part. My wife and I even went to see Louis Mayer and said that I was the perfect scarecrow and insisted that I play it. We finally won out.'

Fortunately Buddy Ebsen was not unduly worried about a change of role as long as he remained in what he was convinced was going to be a 'big picture' and he began to rehearse all over again as the Tin Man. Sadly, his association with the picture was to be short-lived: after two weeks of shooting, and after he had recorded all his songs, he was suddenly taken ill with a chest complaint and rushed to hospital. There it was found that the make-up used to give him the tin effect – aluminium dust sprayed over a layer of white grease paint – had got into his lungs. Though he made a speedy recovery, he was replaced by Jack Haley, who was provided with a new form of make-up.

The whole business of make-up on *The Wizard of Oz* left vivid memories with Ray Bolger:

'We all had trouble with it, because it closed up the pores on our faces and put us in the position that we were unable to work for any great length of time. In fact, when Buddy Ebsen left we had to stop and start all over again, and after that it was so slow shooting in the very, very hot lights, not like those we have today.

'We had no air conditioning and every once in a while we'd have to open these great big doors onto the set. The director Victor Fleming would stop film-making so that we could breathe. Technicolor was a very slow process then and the only thing we did on the set to make ourselves feel like we were not going to die was to joke all the time. We'd play jokes on each other and that way we'd keep our spirits up.'

Bolger's make-up as the Scarecrow was specially devised to resemble the figure drawn by W.W. Denslow in the first of Frank Baum's books. The head, made of rubber to simulate burlap, was tied to his body by a rope, and he wore a broad-brimmed hat that was an exact duplicate of Denslow's original. It took over an hour for the Scarecrow's face – a rubber bag fitted over his head with only holes for his eyes – to be glued on, and then another hour for the brown make-up to be applied. Removing the bag was an equally laborious process, for if the make-up man was careful, it could be used a second and even a third time – in fact, over a hundred masks were used and discarded during the making of *The Wizard of Oz*.

Ray Bolger recalled ruefully that when he took the bag off for the final time at the end of shooting, he discovered that the corners of his mouth and part of his chin had become permanently lined from playing the Scarecrow.

As to his interpretation of the character, he had this to say: 'I kind of made myself go limp. I thought, "I have no bones. I have nothing in me. It's just the wind that's holding me up". I

Bolger filming with Judy Garland on the studio set of *The Wizard of Oz*

walked on the side of my ankles so I would be as floppy as possible. As far as my brain was concerned, I knew I didn't have one. So I had to make a character without a brain but with a logic of a sort, with common sense. And I tried to get a sound in my voice that was complete wonderment – because I was so new, so newly made.'

Bolger also delighted in telling the story of how his song 'If I Only Had A Brain' came to be used. The music had originally been written by Harold Arlen for a musical show *Hooray for What*! where it was called 'I'm Hanging Onto You', but when it was inexplicably discarded he revamped it for *The Wizard of Oz* and E.Y. 'Yip' Harburg, his collaborator on the film score, provided the words.

'I think their contribution to the picture was vitally important,' Bolger said. 'They made a simple philosophy out of the songs. They said that there's no place like home and that everybody has a heart, a brain and courage. Use them properly and you will reach that pot of gold at the end of the rainbow, and that pot of gold is a home. That, in my opinion, has been the secret of the picture's success and longevity.'

At the time of making *The Wizard of Oz*, Bolger was surprised when what he thought was one of his best scenes was dropped: 'It came just where I met Dorothy. It was about ten or fifteen minutes long. I was on wires. The winds came and blew me up in the air and down and up again. It was a fantastic dance. But the thing was it didn't really mean anything overall to the picture. I think now it was right to cut it because it set up a tone that was never followed, a move away from the sort of realistic theatricalism that we used.'

In fact, the sequence lay in the MGM vaults for several decades until it was rediscovered in 1985 and included in a compilation of famous dance routines from films, entitled *That's Dancing*. For many viewers it was the highlight of the picture.

To the end of his days, Ray Bolger was known as 'The World's Favourite Scarecrow', and hundreds of fan letters from young people newly introduced to the magic of Oz continued to arrive at his Beverly Hills home every year. Though he played many other parts he was always grateful for the role that made him famous. Indeed, he kept his Scarecrow costume of coat, hat, gloves, trousers and shoes and donated them to the Smithsonian Institution on his death. Apart from the little piece of immortality he earned on the screen, he also got MGM to agree that any imitation doll of his Scarecrow that was licensed for manufacture would carry a tag bearing the words 'The Scarecrow in *The Wizard of Oz* was played by Ray Bolger' – and by doing so became one of the first stars to enjoy a stake in film merchandising.

'When we made the picture, none of us realized what we were creating,' he said a few months before his death, 'but it's the proudest thing that I've done. This is the thing I'll be remembered for.'

It has been suggested that the eventual success of the 1939 *Wizard of Oz* did much to sustain interest in Frank Baum's books and that, if the film critics' verdict had been proved correct, they might now be no more than curiosities in literary

The famous singer Michael Jackson transformed into the scarecrow in the all-black version of Frank Baum's novel called *The Wiz* (1978)

history instead of landmarks.

It also inspired further film versions of the story, two using actors and another couple using animation.

The first, made in 1978, was a strikingly original variation called *The Wiz*, which was, in effect, an all-black *Wizard of Oz*. The man behind this idea was a young black New York disc jockey, Kenneth Harper, and it was brought to the screen under the guidance of the British director Sidney Lumet, who wrote the script in collaboration with Joel Schumacher. The musical score was written by lyricist and composer Charlie Smalls. Budgeted to cost $12 million, *The Wiz* was finally completed for a staggering $24 million.

Dorothy was portrayed in the picture as a young Harlem kindergarten teacher who is whirled away to a Land of Oz – a harsh parody of the city of New York. Here she falls in with a Cowardly Lion, a Tin Man and a Scarecrow, whom she first meets on a piece of urban wasteland. Together this quartet face the dangers of a jungle-like city, finally triumphing over all the odds.

The singer Diana Ross was cast as Dorothy, with the black comedians Ted Ross and Nipsey Russell playing the Lion and Tin Man respectively. Lena Horne appeared as Glinda the Good Fairy, and the versatile comic Richard Pryor, as the Wiz. The part of the Scarecrow went to a teenaged singer-dancer destined to become a world-wide sensation, Michael Jackson. His performance was certainly unlike any previous attempt at portraying the character: he was loose-limbed and much more nimble and alert than any of his predecessors.

> I have always loved stories of fantasy and magic [Michael Jackson said during filming] and *The Wizard of Oz* was one of my childhood favourites. I thought it was a great idea to update the story and play it against the background of modern-day New York. It is exciting, too, to be working with such a great cast of singers and comedians. They've helped me a lot to get into the role of the straw man.
>
> I have this great scene where Dorothy first meets me. I'm up on a pole and these tough guys, the Crows, are dancing around me, laughing and making fun. It looks as if it was done in the middle of Harlem, but in fact it was shot in the

studio with a lot of special effects. The whole film has that kind of magic about it!

Though the picture was a success at the box-office, the general verdict was that, while it might help sustain the legend, it was a very far cry from the Oz that people knew and loved.

The other recent film version of Baum's story appeared in 1985 from the Walt Disney Organization and was entitled *Return to Oz*. According to popular legend, Disney had wanted to make *The Wizard of Oz* as an animated feature to follow up the great success of *Snow White and the Seven Dwarfs* back in 1937, but MGM secured the rights instead. Then, in 1954, Disney was able to make a deal for the rights to eleven of the Frank Baum books and began to plan a film musical. A first attempt, *The Rainbow Road to Oz*, started filming in February 1958, and a colourful sequence featuring the meeting of the Scarecrow and the Patchwork Girl on the Yellow Brick Road was shot. However, no sooner was this completed than the whole production was halted – for reasons which are still unclear, though it has been suggested that the film-makers were concerned about comparisons being drawn with the Judy Garland picture which was by then triumphantly reaching new audiences on television.

It was not until 1981 that the idea was again revived in the Disney Organization by Walter Murch, a film-maker who had won an Oscar for his work on *Apocalypse Now*. He had been an admirer of Frank Baum's books since childhood and believed that with all the technological wizardry now available it was possible to produce a variation on the old favourite that would be wholly unlike its predecessors.

What Murch did in his script was to combine two Baum stories, *The Land of Oz* and *Ozma of Oz*, into a single story, which retained the four central characters, Dorothy, the Tin Man, the Cowardly Lion and the Scarecrow, and introduced such new faces as the robot Tik-Tok, Jack Pumpkinhead, Billina the chicken and the Gump. In casting the picture, he also took a gamble in choosing a nine-year-old Canadian girl, Fairuza Balik, with just one television appearance behind her, to play Dorothy – the first time a child actress had played the role.

The Walt Disney film, *Return to Oz* (1985) in which dancer Justin Case played an energetic scarecrow whose appearance was based on the illustrations provided by John R. Neil for the Oz sequels – a typical example is shown here

In *Return to Oz* Dorothy finds her friends reduced to stone and has to outwit the Nome King (Nicol Williamson) and Evil Princess (Jean Marsh) to restore them to life. The energetic young actor Justin Case gave a fine performance as the Scarecrow, who is made King of Oz when he is finally re-animated. This Scarecrow's appearance was modelled not on W.W. Denslow's original concept but on the later illustrations provided for Baum's various sequels by John R. Neil.

The film was generally liked by the critics – Alexander Walker of the *London Standard*, for instance, called it a 'brilliantly imaginative movie, breathlessly eventful and endlessly inventive'. He could not, however, rid himself of the conviction that, 'Ultimately, the simple spell exerted by the Judy Garland movie may prove the stronger one.'

The first of the two animated films was *Journey Back To Oz*, an ambitious attempt made by Filmation Associates in 1971 and directed by Hal Sutherland. There were some interesting parallels to be drawn between this ninety-minute colour extravaganza and the 1939 Judy Garland picture. For one, her daughter Liza Minnelli spoke the lines of Dorothy, and Margaret Hamilton, who had appeared as the Wicked Witch, was now transformed into loving Aunt Em. The comedian Milton Berle impersonated the Cowardly Lion, with Danny Thomas as the Tin Man and Mickey Rooney playing a zany Scarecrow who has already been installed as the King of Oz when the little girl from Kansas arrives in the magic kingdom to help him defeat a plan by the evil Mombi to dethrone him. Unforgettable, too, was that man of a million voices, Mel Blanc, as Crow.

In 1982 the Japanese studio of Toho released *The Wizard of Oz*, an animated feature in colour running for seventy-eight minutes and shown in America in 1982. Crudely drawn, the film bears a strong similarity to the typical Japanese cartoon tales of super-heroes battling fiendish intergalactic foes than to Frank Baum's fantasy classic. The Wizard, for instance, possesses the most unimaginable power at his fingertips, while the Scarecrow is able not only to change his shape at will but to breathe fire on his enemies!

*

The cartoon version of the scarecrow as he appeared in *Journey Back To Oz* made in 1971

Other cartoon films in recent years featuring scarecrows have done rather better by the scarecrow.

Columbia Pictures' *Crop Chasers* (1953), for example, featured two meek little scarecrows, terrorized by gangster-like crows, who win over their enemies by saving a baby crow from drowning. The popular Barney Bear in the story of *Joe Scarecrow* (Columbia, 1968) enlisted the aid of the seemingly helpful Joe to scare off the crows from his farm only to find that his helper is actually two crows in disguise!

Scarecrow Adventure (Kingston Films, 1975) concerned a scarecrow who is unhappy with the nickname 'Demon Dan' given him by a farmer's children, and earns himself a more friendly sobriquet after rescuing a tiny rabbit from a predatory bird. *Scarecrow* (1976), a Hungarian production, was a delightful cameo featuring a male and a female scarecrow who come to life in a field and dance a joyous polka together.

Most recently, *Scarecrow*, from Zagreb Films of Yugoslavia, released in 1986, was an animated fantasy in which a scarecrow and the crows who plague his life are finally made to settle their differences when one of the birds is hurt and the scarecrow provides the shelter and comfort in which the creature can recover.

Also in recent years some imaginative short films about the scarecrow have appeared, further underlining the figure's cinematic possibilities.

In 1962 the Yugoslavia Film Company made a ten-minute film called *Scarecrow* which featured a real scarecrow in a field. The picture was very much a mood-piece for children, showing a day in the life of the central character from dawn to dusk. Two years later the East German DEFA Studios offered a twenty-four minute colour production called *The Scarecrow* directed by Lutz Kohleft. This was a modern ballet set to the music of Dvořák about a jilted girl who gets her revenge on her rival by dressing up as a scarecrow. The picture was first screened in the West at the Edinburgh Film Festival in 1964.

A highly dramatic piece of film-making, *Scarecrow*, conceived, written and directed by John Sharrad for the British Film Institute in 1972, was first shown at the Edinburgh Film Festival in 1973 and received considerable acclaim. It seems, in hindsight, to have been the forerunner of a batch of film and television productions playing on the scarecrow's sinister qualities. Though Sharrad's film runs a bare seventeen minutes, its atmosphere of mounting terror and ultimate tragedy seems to grip the viewer for far longer.

The story is set in Ireland in the early 1930s at the height of a drought and tells of the desperate efforts of a poor farmer to save his crops from the ravages of rooks. Although he has constructed a number of weird scarecrows which stand about the landscape like black sentinels, still the birds mock him unless he stays in the fields himself and shoots them relentlessly with his gun.

Don Blackwell as the farmer persecuted into madness by scarecrows in John Sharrad's dramatic movie, *Scarecrow* (1972)

Gradually the farmer's vigil in the scorching sunlight turns into a nightmare. The scarecrows stir and seem to move about the fields of their own volition. At this, the man begins to fire wildly at everything in sight – especially the scarecrows, who now loom all about him, thrusting their skinny arms at him whichever way he turns.

Finally the camera reveals that not only has the farmer killed all the rooks but in his madness he has shot down members of his family. The film closes with a sudden downpour of rain and the stricken man standing amidst the terrible carnage that he has wreaked.

That year also saw the release of *Scarecrow*, an X-rated feature-length film directed by Jerry Schatzberg and starring Gene Hackman and Al Pacino which won the year's Cannes Film Festival Grand Prix Award. The story, by Garry Michael White, concerns two down-at-heel drifters, Max (Hackman) and Lion (Pacino), who strike up an unlikely friendship while hitch-hiking across the back roads of America and plan to try to find a better life for themselves. Instead, their association ends in tragedy.

Jay Cocks of *Time* magazine explained the relevance of the film title to its story in these words: 'Max and Lion's progress across the country is not so much geographical as spiritual. Max likes to whore and brawl: Lion sees himself as a scarecrow. "Those crows don't bother the field because they're scared of the scarecrow". Lion tries to live a life of casual but crafty comedy. Max is skeptical, reminding Lion that "you're not playing with a full deck. You've got one foot in the great beyond".'

Trevor Hyett of the *Morning Star* put it slightly differently: 'Scarecrows don't scare away the crows, they just make them laugh. So the crows say to themselves, "Hey! That old farmer can't be such a bad guy, he's made us laugh ... let's leave his seed alone". At least in *Scarecrow* this is the assertion of young Lion as he tried to convince Max to confront life with a smile and not with his fists.'

An even more scarecrow-like figure emerged in 1982 in the form of John Carradine, the cadaverous star of dozens of horror films, who played the central character in yet another film called *The Scarecrow*. Produced in New Zealand and directed by Sam Pillsbury from Ronald Hugh Morrison's

John Carradine, looking for all the world like a ragged scarecrow, in the highly-acclaimed New Zealand movie, *The Scarecrow* (1982)

classic novel of 'Mystery, Mirth and Murder', the story tells of the terrible events that overwhelm a small town following the arrival of a sinister stranger.

Describing the picture, the *Scotsman*'s critic William Darante wrote: 'Into this colourful community comes the Scarecrow figure of magician, Hubert Salter (Carradine). It is clear to the spectator that this vagrant amalgam of straggling hair, twisted limbs and conjuring tricks is the perpetrator of a series of local murders. But none of the inhabitants seems to notice....'

The Scarecrow comes across as a mixture of horror, black farce and folksy domesticity as Slater orchestrates a series of grisly events, and it was perhaps not surprising that Tom Hutchinson of the *Daily Mail* felt moved to comment in his review that, 'Despite Worzel Gummidge, scarecrows have never had a good Press.' He continued: 'Their flapping semblance of humanity, intended to scare birds, can so easily send our own goose-pimples squawking. So this film by calling its central character The Scarecrow intends an added frisson with that title, as the ageing sex-maniac stalks young girls in a small backwoods town in the 1950s.'

In singling out the performance of John Carradine for particular praise, Monty Smith of *New Musical Express* added: 'One classic image will live with me forever. The Scarecrow himself standing on the railway station, one second as large and still as life in the platform's shadows, the next completely enshrouded by the steam from a passing train.'

Brutal events in a small rural community were also the focus of *Dark Night of the Scarecrow*, starring Charles Dunning, made in 1981 by the now famous American horror film director Frank de Felitta (*Halloween* and *Friday the 13th*) from an original story by J.D. Feigelson.

The film describes what happens when a little country girl is found covered in blood and nearly dead, and the immediate assumption is drawn that the child's severely retarded man-friend, Bubba, is responsible. A group of vigilantes go after the unfortunate and, finding him hiding inside a scarecrow, kill him. But Bubba was innocent and had actually saved the girl from a vicious dog. The men then stand trial for murder but are freed through lack of evidence.

Nevertheless, Bubba's spirit seeks revenge ...

In 1986 a frightening scarecrow also appeared briefly in another controversial production, Dennis Potter's six-part BBC television serial *The Singing Detective*, starring Michael Gambon. This many-faceted story of a hack writer inflicted with a skin disease and burdened with guilt feelings from his past made compulsively watchable television. The final episode featured a terrifying schoolmistress who had plagued the young man's childhood and suddenly turned into an even more terrifying scarecrow, relentlessly pursuing him no matter which way he turned. Janet Henfrey, who endowed the schoolmistress with such venom, made an equally impressive scarecrow – perhaps the best ever portrayed by a woman.

It is also on television, of course, that the most famous of all scarecrows, Worzel Gummidge, continues to make his presence felt in what seems likely to be a long-running series of adventures, played by the versatile Jon Pertwee. But though the former radio star and third 'Doctor Who' is now very much identified with the role, he was not the first to play Gummidge on TV.

In fact, Worzel Gummidge made his debut on the small screen back in 1953, when his creator, Barbara Euphan Todd, was still alive, and when television was in its infancy. In June that year Queen Elizabeth II was crowned and the spectacle was relayed to millions of viewers; that same month Worzel Gummidge made his debut as part of 'Children's Television'.

The person responsible for bringing the scarecrow from Scatterbrook Farm to the small screen was Joy Harrington, the producer of children's serials at the BBC and a friend of Barbara Euphan Todd. The scripts for the series, called simply *Worzel Gummidge*, were written jointly by Joy Harrington and Barbara Euphan Todd, who also consulted together in casting actors to play the various roles. For Earthy Mangold, Worzel's wife, they had no hesitation in calling on Mabel Constanduros, who had frequently played the part in the radio versions. In both appearance and voice she matched the part perfectly.

Among the same group of performers who had starred in

THE STRAW MAN ON THE SCREEN

Television's first Worzel Gummidge, Frank Atkinson, with Mabel Constanduros as Earthy Mangold, in BBC TV's production *Worzel Gummidge Turns Detective* made in 1953

the radio adaptation, they also found the right man to play Worzel, the versatile Frank Atkinson, who had played Mr Braithwaite, the farmer, and occasionally one of Worzel's scarecrow friends, Bogle.

'I was very familiar with Barbara Euphan Todd's stories so I suppose that was part of the reason why I was asked to play Worzel,' Atkinson reminisced some time after the stories had been screened. 'That and the fact I came from a country background and had seen plenty of scarecrows about when I was a child. My Worzel was rather different from the character shown in the books, though. I had a greatcoat with a turned-up collar and a battered bowler hat on my head. I also wore a sort of skull cap which covered everything except my eyes, nose and mouth, and this was supposed to represent sackcloth. It often itched a bit – but nowhere near as much as the real straw I had stuffed around my collar and up my sleeves and trousers!'

The adventures of Worzel Gummidge were all made at the BBC studios at Lime Grove on sets built to represent Scatterbrook Farm and the field in which Worzel and Earthy stood.

'The stories lasted half an hour each,' Frank recalled, 'and they went out live. We had to be word perfect and not miss a cue. Although the two main sets were not far apart, it was sometimes a bit of a scramble to get from one to the other in time – especially if you were faded out at the end of one scene and had to appear immediately at the start of the next one somewhere else!'

'The series was very popular with young viewers and I got lots of letters from children who said I looked just as they had always imagined Worzel to be,' Frank added. 'And in a way I was surprised the BBC didn't do more than one series. I always felt the old scarecrow was a character with endless possibilities!'

It was not until almost a quarter of a century later that another actor brought Worzel back to the screen. This revival was by a commerical television company, Southern Television, rather than the BBC, and again it was a series – but the first intention had been to make a large-screen film, as actor Jon Pertwee recalls:

'The film producer Gareth Wigan approached me and said that he wanted to make a movie of Worzel Gummidge and would I play the part? He'd already got those wonderfully talented writers Keith Waterhouse and Willis Hall, who created *Billy Liar*, to write a script, and it didn't take me a moment to make up my mind. Well, I'd loved the books as a child so I jumped at the chance. But surprisingly we couldn't get the financial backing and so the film idea fell through.'

However, Jon Pertwee was convinced Worzel could be a hit on television and, after an initial refusal from Thames Television, the idea was taken up by Southern. His own enthusiasm for the role transmitted itself to everyone involved in

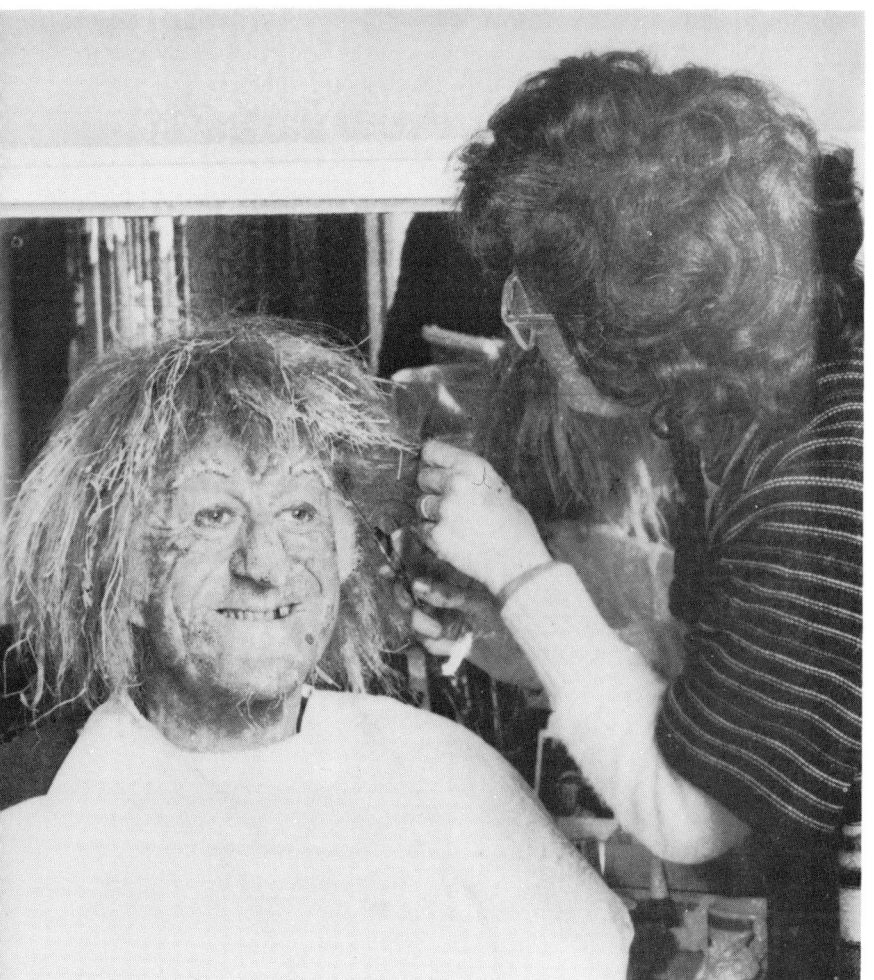

A behind-the-scenes photograph of the transformation of Jon Pertwee into the rascally Worzel Gummidge

the first series of seven stories.

'Worzel was my baby,' he explained in an interview given after this opening series had been transmitted in 1979. 'I created it, and it's by far the best thing I have ever done. It's a dream part, in fact. He's sullen, touching, vulgar, rude, smelly, with not one redeeming feature. What's more, he really is in love with the most objectionable woman ever! Of course, he's a fantasy figure, but he sincerely believes in himself. He's also evil, wicked, but lovable and all that makes for sadness as well as fun. He has you in tears.'

What Jon Pertwee and the Waterhouse-Hall partnership had done was to transform Worzel from just a children's storybook character into an irascible reprobate whom adults could enjoy watching too. Other changes included turning Aunt Sally (played by Una Stubbs) from Worzel's aunt into the woman the scarecrow wants to marry, despite her nasty nature, and having the two children (Jeremy Austin and Charlotte Barton) now being looked after by a none-too-successful father rather than a nanny.

Why did Jon Pertwee think he had proved such a good choice as Worzel? 'Well, I'm a sort of decadent string bean type as an actor and I have an ear for dialect,' he said. 'Being brought up in Devonshire I also picked up the kind of accent I could use for Worzel. In fact, I have used many of my childhood experiences in creating the character of Gummidge. Worzel goes into a sulk if he doesn't get what he wants, but also if he is misunderstood – which was a reason I sulked when I was younger as I was terribly over-sensitive.

'I'm terribly short-tempered and so is Worzel. I didn't accept to play Worzel because he was like me, but it happened to work out that he is.'

Authenticity was very much a keynote in the making of the series, and a farm at Braishfield, a pretty village near Romsey in Hampshire was used for location shooting. At a cost of approximately £60,000 per episode, the Southern TV series was a considerable improvement on the earlier studio-bound BBC version.

Jon Pertwee took a great deal of care over his make-up as Worzel. To make his face look like a humanized worzel (a type of turnip), a carrot was used to extend his nose, hairs from carrot tops were used for a scraggy beard, sugar puffs were stuck in strategic positions to make warts, and horsehair, raffia and barley were used for his wig. Plaited corn provided the scarecrow's eyebrows, his teeth were painted with black and brown enamel to give the appearance of decay, and his face was liberally splattered with mud.

Perhaps Jon Pertwee's greatest achievement, though, was the creation of 'Worzelese', his scarecrow language.

Just a few of the promotions which have featured Worzel Gummidge in recent years

'Right at the start I wanted this new language for Worzel,' he explains. 'Well, we all sat down one morning and began thinking in "Scarecrow" terms. Then after a fruitless half an hour we realised we were going about it the wrong way. We should be thinking in "Worzel" terms. Once we'd established that Worzel should be the centrepiece of the language it all began to string together.

'Suddenly it became a matter of putting a "Wor" in between each letter of every word, and ending them with "Zel". But then we found that didn't have enough variations – there had to be something else to increase the interest, to make it sound a little more intricate than it actually was. And so we decided to end words with four letters or over with "Zel", but what to do with words of up to three letters? It was important to get the right *sound*. It had to be a *hard* sound rather than a soft one. We came up with dozens from "Dig" to "Dill' and "Mig" to "Zig", but in the end we liked "Dip" the most. Thus Worzelese was born.'

Worzel's universal appeal has also been applied in various forms of merchandising, such as games, posters and annuals, a long-playing record, 'Worzel Sings' and musical Christmas show, as well as the use of the scarecrow's likeness in several special promotions ranging from one for a chain of restaurants to another for a well-known brand of breakfast cereal.

Jon Pertwee believes Worzel's popularity still has far to go, and he intends to continue playing him on television for some years yet. 'It was very much a gamble for me taking the part in the first place, my professional pride and faith in myself would have been shattered if it hadn't worked. So I still reckon I owe the old reprobate another year or two of my life!'

This continuing success of Worzel Gummidge would no doubt surprise Barbara Euphan Todd if she were still alive today, for she set out originally with no greater ambition than to weave some entertaining tales around the scarecrow – and yet by so doing has proved it to be one of the most attractive figures to be found anywhere in the countryside.

5 The Twentieth-Century Scarecrow

'These upstart scarecrows of the wand'ring skies.'
                                    THOMAS BROWN

Ever since I was a child I have never been able to resist taking a close look at any scarecrow I have come across – no matter if it stands in the middle of a large field or in a small back garden. Nor does it worry me unduly whether it is a tatty, bedraggled specimen or a sprucely clothed and upstanding member of the fraternity, for both represent a conscientious piece of work on someone's part as well as a belief in an enduring country tradition.

There is also to be savoured what I can only describe as a mixture of excitement and apprehension about approaching a scarecrow, for the best of them can give the illusion of being very human-like until one gets right up close. And sometimes even then the sudden stirring of the wind can cause them to move in such a way as to turn apprehension into unease. The sceptic may say that the birds have long had the upper hand over the scarecrow, but why, then, do so many country people, farmers included, still make them and set them up on their fields?

The evidence that they still do – and not only in Britain but elsewhere in the world – is there to be seen for anyone who cares to look. I know, because that is precisely what I have been doing for some years now.

One of the most striking examples of the durability of the tradition I have come across occurred during the very year I was writing this book – 1987 – when my family and I happened to visit Stratford-on-Avon, the birthplace of William Shakespeare, whose association with the scarecrow I have already outlined in some detail. While we were touring the town on an open-top bus, passing along Chapel Lane close to the site of New Place where the playwright lived for a number of years, what should we spy on a smallholding but an unmistakable figure keeping patient vigil over rows of vegetables. A most vivid example of how a 300-year-old custom was still being observed!

Elsewhere in Warwickshire other scarecrows substantiate the fact that this was no isolated exception. For example, we spotted several in the fields around Broadway, a Cotswold village with lines of weathered, stone-built houses. There was one splendid fellow, in a field of sugarbeet not far from Broadway Tower, dressed in the very latest attire: a zip-up red overall suit!

Across the border in Gloucestershire in the curiously named little village of Lower Slaughter not far from Stow-in-the-Wold, I came across another modern member of the fraternity dressed in the extraordinary combination of dungarees and the jacket of a morning suit. Shaded from the sun by a floppy hat (and carrying an umbrella hung over one arm in case of rain), he bore a slogan which indicated he had been placed in a garden 'Sown with Grass and Wild Flowers'. From the evidence of the flora growing all around him, he was obviously doing a good job.

Elsewhere the story is the same. An even more dramatic-looking figure than the one at Lower Slaughter was spotted not so long ago by Henry Maskell, when he was passing through Oxley in Shropshire.

'Imagine my surprise,' he wrote, 'when I saw a scarecrow with a real gun, an old-fashioned muzzle loader, and the barrel shining without a speck of rust! The holder of the gun sat at his ease on a real chair not far from a cottage door, and there was something ferocious in the gleam of his bloodshot eyes, and the cruel sardonic mouth that creased his calico countenance from ear to ear. A splendid crop of peas bore token to his vigilance.'

Mr Maskell's friend A.L. Collins took the opportunity to sketch this redoubtable figure, and his illustration appears here.

In the West Country, too, scarecrows are very much a part of the landscape, as W.O.G. Lofts reported to me in a letter recently:

A.L. Collins' fine portrait of a scarecrow armed with a blunderbuss that he saw in Shropshire!

One day when I was in the West Country I visited an old farmer and found him in his kitchen with some sort of mechanical contraption which had clearly gone wrong. Knowing that I had once been an engineer, he asked if I could

Humorous drawings by Terry Willers of Irish scarecrows including a County Clare scarecrow looking like President Eamon De Valera, one of the popular Irish sporting scarecrows, and The Merry Mayoman who featured in an extraordinary court case!

mend his 'scarecrow', as he called it. Apparently, when set up in the field the machine had a time clock that fired off loud reports to scare away the birds.

What had happened was that the timing device had gone wrong and it was now making a terrible din at all the wrong times. Even in the middle of the night – which was not making him very popular with his neighbours! Unfortunately, though, the machine was not something in my line, so I suggested that he return it to the manufacturer and get it expertly repaired.

He looked at me and nodded his head. 'Well, it's back to the old scarecrow,' he said in his broad Devonshire accent. 'You can't beat them, really.'

These sympathies can also be heard echoed in East Anglia, where I live and where the scarecrow is much in evidence. The former BBC personality and nature lover John Timpson, writing in his column 'Rural Man' in the *Daily Mail* of 8 May 1987, said: 'My neighbour still relies on the traditional scarecrow. It looks like it has moved on a bit since the Worzel Gummidge era – it has a better class of clothing these days, and instead of a turnip and some straw it has a face like Adolf Hitler, which is disconcerting for passers-by, if not the birds!'

The writer and illustrator Pip Miller of Norwich has also gathered plentiful evidence of hardy scarecrows at work in the fields of East Anglia during her travels, drawing and photographing the rural scene. He researches further underline both the variety and ingenuity which go into the making of scarecrows – no two I have ever come across have been quite alike!

However, if variety is the spice of life for *English* scarecrows, it is doubly so in Ireland, where a leading writer on country topics, Cormac MacConnell, recently conducted a nation-wide survey and reported his findings in an essay entitled 'Men of Straw' published in the magazine *Cara* in 1985:

> Irish scarecrows are no mere scarecrows. They are unique social structures, all the tribes and clans of them, from the Stooping Skibbereen Scarecrow to the Merry Mayoman. From the Lesser Longford Scarecrow to the Donegal Dandy, from the One-Armed Antrim Scarecrow to the Armed

Wexfordman, and from the Long John Silvers of Sligo to the Napoleon Scarecrows of North Tipperary, entirely without arms, brooding over Brussel sprouts and runner beans that didn't run fast enough to escape the rooks. Oh yes, unique social structures, all peculiar to their own place. Typical of their topography, evocative of their environment, mirrors of the mores of their makers. The Scariff Scarecrows of County Clare, great gaunt giants, still bear an almost uncanny resemblance to the late President Eamon De Valera, founder father of the nation, local favourite son for fifty generations of scarecrows.

According to Cormac MacConnell, Irish scarecrows are much more than 'fowl frighteners' and should be regarded as another index to Irish individuality. They are in no way like the 'regimented' English scarecrows – as he somewhat unfairly refers to them – or those from America and Europe, which he also a little inaccurately claims 'come unendingly from the land of Oz'.

'In such company,' he goes on, 'the Irish scarecrow is Ozymandias, king of kings. The Armed Wexfordman, for example, actually comes alive one day each season, causing fearful execution. He is the fellow placed in the corner of the strawberry gardens, kneeling like a fowler, a stick, shotgun-like to the shoulder. The hungry young crows come to despise him. And then one dawn the cunning farmer, with a genuine shotgun, takes the scarecrow's place, with dire results for the raiders.'

Every area of the nation has its own kind of scarecrow, MacConnell says. It may take years to recognize them all, but there are general regional trends which can be used as starting points. For example:

> The clans of Munster scarecrows by and large are small. They are expected to guard large areas, are placed in postures indicating ongoing hard labour, are equipped with caps, and frequently have no trousers at all! Ulster scarecrows are the largest of all, of forbidding appearance, always face towards Mother England, and normally have only one arm.
>
> The scarecrows of Leinster are a motley lot, difficult to categorise, but they frequently have two arms spread wide apart, almost as if inviting birds to attack their fertile gardens,

and, with the exception of the raffish, unique Donegal Dandies, are the best-dressed scarecrows in the country. Sometimes they even have three-piece suits! The really ragged and rascally scarecrows are to be found in Connacht. They are the fattest, sometimes have only one leg, and unfailingly wear a hat and overcoat.

According to MacConnell's findings, Irish scarecrows are also regularly involved in sport and politics. If any football or hurling team wins a championship, the local scarecrows often end up in club jerseys. Some have carried posters supporting candidates in local elections – one or two of their number paying the ultimate price for their loyalty.

Cormac MacConnell's best scarecrow story, however, concerns one he saw in court.

> He was a Merry Mayoman, and he was dragged into the courthouse by two strong policemen. The Sergeant even removed the Mayoman's battered black hat as he was kept upstanding on his two timber legs before the Bench as the case unfolded. It was a poteen case.
>
> The main State witness told how he paid the moonshiner £4 but wasn't actually given the moonshine. He was told, instead, to search the scarecrow's right hand overcoat pocket on his way home. Inside he found the bottle of poteen. The defence successfully argued that the moonshiner, the alleged defendant, hadn't supplied the poteen; it was the scarecrow.
>
> The learned Justice, a man with a fine sense both of law and of fun, dismissed the case against the moonshiner and gave the scarecrow the benefit of the Probation Act. He then went on to warn other scarecrows to mind their own business and not to engage themselves in human enterprises of any kind!

In Scotland, too, the scarecrow is looked upon with a mixture of interest and amusement. It is widely known north of the border by the name of 'tattie-bogle', and there are a number of stories and poems on record which indicate the kind of affection in which it is held. Take, for example, the following dialect verses written by the Glasgow poet W.D. Crocker in 1932:

THE TWENTIETH-CENTURY SCARECROW

A Scottish Tattie-Bogle on duty in Perthshire

Drumduff had a dine tattie-bogle,
Unmarrowed on neebourin' ferms,
A graip was his stumpie wee body,
The shank o' a besom his airms;
An' we buskit him braw for a bogle
No' tatter'd, but tosh-like and spruce,
Though his class were a wee thing auld-farrant,
Victorian – or Robert the Bruce.
On his neep heid a lum hat was cockit,
An' he wore a wee sarkie wi' frills,
He could fricht ony crow in the parish,
As he stood, a' his lane, 'mang the drills.

A gangrel cam' by in the gloamin';
As he hirpled ower-by tae the ferm,
He thocht a fair swap o' their raiment
Would dae him an' the bogle nae herm;
Sae his clarty auld duds he sune strippit,
I'se warrant the chiel had some cause,
For quo' he, 'This auld sark I was wearin'
Frichts me, sae it's shair tae fricht craws!'
He has niffr'd his sark we' the bogle

His breeks, coat and bunnet forby;
An' he's aff wi' lum hat and frill'd sarkie,
As prood as a piper frae Skye.

The gude-man cam' hame by the munelicht,
At the clachan they keepit him late,
Wi' the dram in his heid he was singin',
Though he kent hoo tae gang the richt gate.
But the sang feenished aff wi' skirl –
Oh! could he believe his ain een? –
For through the slap, walkin' tae meet him
His ain tattie-bogle was seen
Quo' the gudeman, 'Gude save an' preserve us!
I'se never again tak' a dram'
He shook, his kees chappit thegither
Syne he cowp'd in the sheuch in a dwam.

The neebours heard tell o' the story
An losh, but they tgocht it a baur,
They said, 'Shairly ane o' your smeddum
Could face tattie-boggles an' waur'
The gudeman jist grued an' said naethin',
For the gudewife had flytit him sair,
But his freens aye kep' lauchin' an' daffin
'Haud your wheesht then,' he cried, 'say nae mair
I've as muckle spunk in me as ony
The thing would ne'er fash'd me ava,
But, gin bogles are noo resurrect'it,
They'll be howkin' oot mithers-in-law!'

Willie Soutar, a Perth poet, also penned evocative lines to the 'tattie-bogle':

The Tattie-Bogle waves his arms,
Caw! Caw! Caw!
He has no bones or intestines,
Caw! Caw! Caw!
We crows who have given attention,
And flapped and starved aslant,
Now go home laughing over the stretch of coarse grass,
Caw! Caw! Caw!

The Scottish scarecrow has featured in some amusing stories. One from the *Campbelltown Courier* (sent to me in October 1986 by Murdo MacDonald, archivist of the Argyll & Bute District Council) is noteworthy because it confirms

THE TWENTIETH-CENTURY SCARECROW 155

the use of scarecrows in the Highlands:

> Southend had a sensation of an uncommon kind last week [the newspaper reported]. On Friday, a message came post haste to the village that a case of suicide had evidently taken place near the Mull, the body of a man being seen swinging from a rope over the cliffs.
>
> At once there was an informal roll call, each man eager to satisfy himself that his neighbour was not missing. The conclusion come to was that some way-farer must have tired of existence.
>
> Some men then set off for the place to investigate, with the result that the alarm was found to be groundless, having been caused by an innocent looking scarecrow which the gamekeeper had dangling over the cliff for the purpose of preventing the hawks from nesting there

While it is evident that most Scottish tattie-bogles are made of cast-off clothing, there has recently been a new species reported made wholly from plastic bags tied to poles fitted with cross-trees. This type apparently originated in the district of Scone and proved most effective because of their lightness and the fact that even the gentlest wind made them

A fearsome French tableau of scarecrows photographed by Neill Menneer at Vaucluse near Avignon

appear very animated. Following publicity in the *Scots Magazine*, similar tattie-bogles were reported to have been seen in eastern Scotland and a few in the islands of the north.

These scarecrows bear a certain similarity to those which have been used for a number of years in France. In Provence, scarecrows tied with ribbons or holding out long strips of plastic which rustle continuously in the breeze have been observed on a number of farms.

As a whole, though, the French believe that the most effective scarecrows are those with hideous faces. Although in most other countries features are scarcely considered important at all, the French often use masks of the Devil or (of late) even the vampire Count Dracula. No wonder the country people love to tell stories about late-night revellers receiving the shocks of their lives from scarecrows apparently leering horribly at them over hedges!

Sometimes, too, groups of scarecrows are arranged in such a way that they look like people at work. This is a favourite recourse of farmers in the south of France defending their young crops from birds. One such group operating a tractor was recently spotted at Vaucluse near Avignon, and a photograph of this extraordinary tableau is reprinted here.

Spanish and Portuguese farmers have also adopted the idea of attaching long trailing pieces of plastic to their scarecrows to give them greater effectiveness. The Portuguese have an old superstition that the best scarecrows are those made entirely of straw, especially straw reaped from an outstanding harvest.

In Germany it is said that the fatter the scarecrow the better will be the protection it provides, and it is also believed to be bad luck to destroy a scarecrow once the harvest has been brought in. It should be carefully stored away in a dry barn for the winter and then returned to the fields – complete with a new set of clothes – as soon as the new year's ploughing has taken place.

In Austria some farmers believe in getting the land and their scarecrows blessed by the local priest at the start of each year in order to ensure they have good crops. In Italy it was a popular belief for years that no scarecrow should ever be dressed in the clothes of someone who had died – ideally they should be the cast-offs of a young man in the prime of life so that some of his vitality might be passed on to the guardian of the fields.

THE TWENTIETH-CENTURY SCARECROW 157

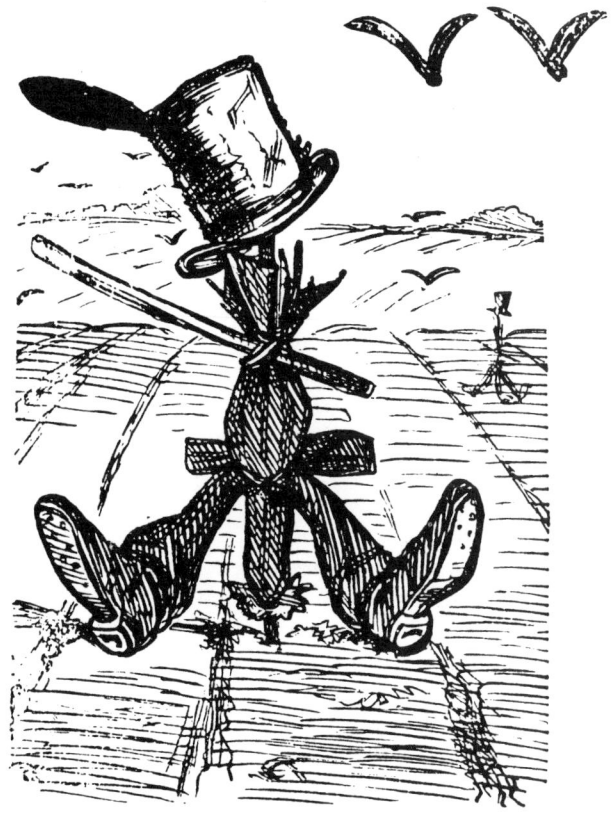

Russian satirical cartoon featuring a scarecrow from *Krokodil* magazine, March 1968

The scarecrow is also in use behind the Iron Curtain. In Hungary great store is placed upon making it as life-like as possible, and carved wooden dummies form the basis of many of these effigies. The facial features are also strikingly good, and once again it is not unusual to hear of cases of mistaken identity when what seemed like the figure of a man stepping out across a field turned out to be nothing but a scarecrow with his clothes blowing in the wind.

Hungarian shepherds have also long observed a custom of placing their sticks in the ground close to their herds and then hanging their coats and hats on them to 'watch over' the sheep while they slip away for a meal or a drink. An analogy here with the scarecrow as 'guardian' of the seed seems very probable.

The Soviet Union's scarecrows have a tendency to be much bigger than those anywhere else because of the enormous Siberian crows which are now widespread across a large part of the country and which have even reached the cities. These grey-black birds can be up to a foot long and, with their harsh cawing, are fearsome. Apart from feeding on corn seed, they will also attack and kill small animals. In the cities these birds have been tackled by guns and poison, but in the rural communities scarecrows up to twelve feet high with arms that whirl around in the wind have had to be built by the peasant farmers. These people are apparently reluctant to engage in wholesale slaughter of the giant crows because of an old adage that to kill one heralds a year of misfortune.

The scarecrow is by no means unknown in Africa, though it has been seen less there since the exodus of white farmers from many of the emergent black nations. Even when scarecrows were used, it was never easy to gauge their efficiency because – as one ex-Colonial told me – any scarecrow dressed in half-way decent clothes would soon be stripped by the natives, who had few clothes themselves and saw no reason why a straw man should be better dressed.

Some Australian and New Zealand farmers have similarly carried on the scarecrow tradition brought out to those countries by their British forebears. Like the Irish scarecrow, the scarecrow Down Under is usually created with a fair amount of humour in his make-up – politicians and sports stars being the inspiration of many a scarecrow found rakishly propped up in the wheat and vegetable fields.

Japanese farmers have been known to use human images not unlike the traditional scarecrow for protecting their crops. An amusing cartoon of a gun-carrying farmer being startled by his own scarecrow is reproduced here from a Japanese satirical magazine.

The United States, with its population originally drawn from many countries of Europe, naturally enough has a thriving scarecrow tradition. As far as records go, there is mention of the use of scarecrows back in 1826 in *The Farm Book* by Thomas Jefferson, a president who farmed at Monticello near Charlottesville in Virginia and who apparently used three scarecrows in his fields of maize and corn.

THE TWENTIETH-CENTURY SCARECROW

Japanese cartoon of a farmer frightened by his own scarecrow!

At least as old as this book is a tradition in the USA that on the night of Halloween (31 October) scarecrows come alive a fact illustrated with grim effect on the cover of the short story magazine *Fear!* which is reproduced in these pages. This superstition is just one of several that has made the last night of October very popular with young children, who prowl about in fancy costumes dressed like ghosts or demons threatening 'Trick or Treat' on their neighbours. Anyone foolish enough to ignore this imprecation is likely to be on the receiving end of a practical joke.

The term 'scarecrow' has also given rise to some curious expressions in America. A 'scare head', for instance, is a

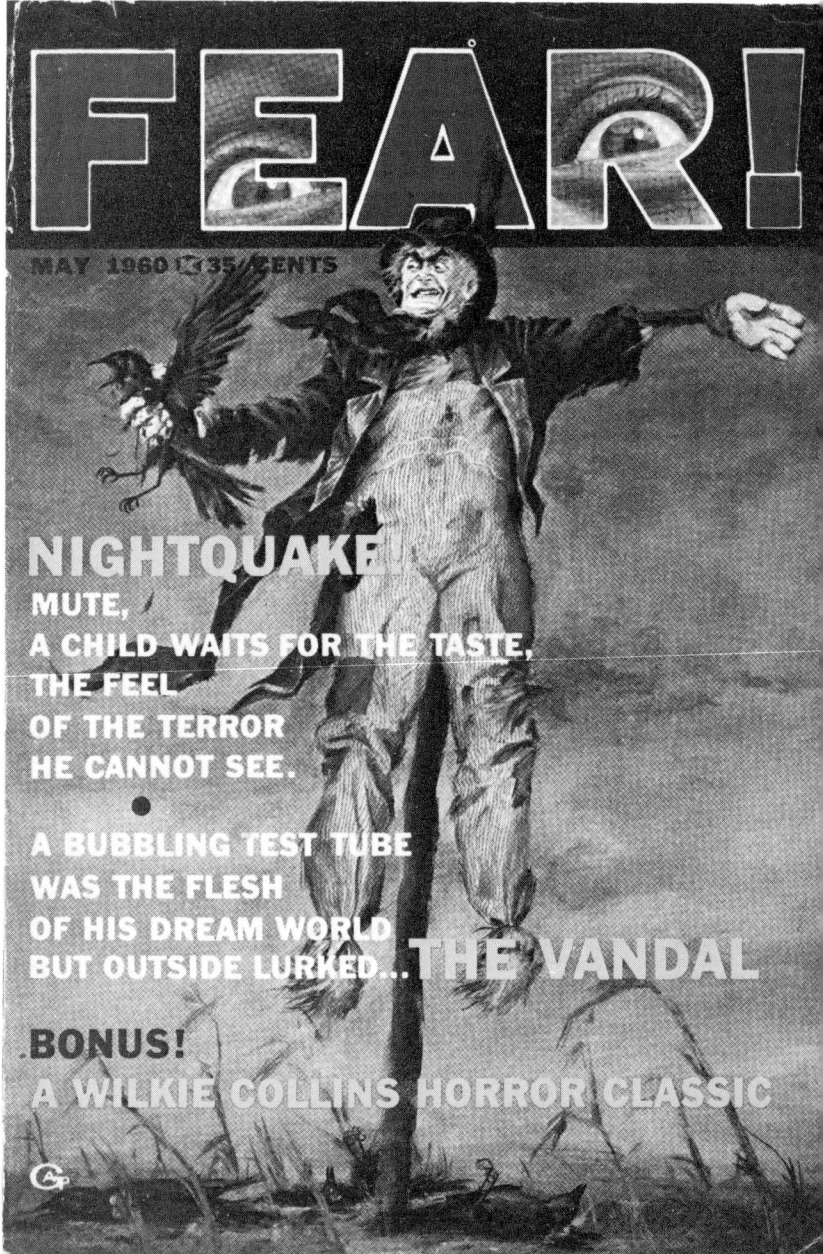

In some American states it is believed that scarecrows come alive on the night of Halloween (31 October), as this chilling front cover of *Fear!* magazine, May 1960, graphically illustrates

newspaper headline of a sensational nature, while the expression 'scaresome' means any frightful sight. In 1846 a 'scare fly' was announced which was said to be a device for scaring away flies. Commented one newspaper, the *Xenia Torch-Light*, rather aptly in its issue of 23 April: 'We have seen many a scare-crow, but never before a *scare fly*!'

In the farming communities of the Mid-West the scarecrow still flourishes today, though, according to a *New York Times* report on 13 April 1981, a new type of scarecrow has been developed for use in cities to protect the seeds of valuable flowers and plants, which is equipped with a video camera instead of a head to warn market gardeners of any approaching feathered marauders.

New developments are occurring almost annually now as far as the scarecrow is concerned – perhaps the most notable being the number of women scarecrows appearing in the fields. Despite the fact that Cormac MacConnell, the Irish researcher, insisted in his 1985 article that, 'Nowhere in the nation will you find a woman scarecrow', in England this is certainly not the case.

For centuries it has quite evidently been believed that the more aggressive image of the male was better suited to frightening off birds, but nowadays it seems the subtler charms but undeniable strength of character of women can be equally effective.

The cynic might argue that, as women by and large buy more clothes than men, they have more cast-offs for use in the making of scarecrows. Also, women's clothes are looser and blow about more readily in the breeze, thereby creating an even more animated birdscarer.

Although there have certainly been women scarecrows in British fields for many years, it is only in recent times that they have become really evident. The first significant use seems to have been in the early 1930s, and this may well have followed a feature on the topic in the *Guardian* (or *Manchester Guardian* as it was then) of 8 February 1933. The story, headlined unobtrusively 'The Scarecrow', was written by a staff writer, Orgill MacKenzie, and used an imaginary countrywoman, 'Mrs Cumming', to argue the case for female scarecrows, following a report of two such creations being spotted in the fields of Cheshire.

Scarecrows equipped with video cameras instead of heads to keep a watch out for marauding birds are the latest development in America!

'Mrs Cumming', explained Orgill MacKenzie, had grown increasingly frustrated by the inability of her 'male' scarecrow to drive off the birds that were pillaging her pea crops and cherry trees. He went on:

> Mrs Cumming frowned at the nature of her problem, and then suddenly her features resumed their amiable disposition. 'There's no reason,' she said to herself, 'why a scarecrow should be a man.' And she went at once to forage in her wardrobe, where there were plenty of clothes for scarecrows, and found a boat-shaped hat and an old tweed suit, too wide in the skirt, too tight in the waist.
>
> She spent a happy morning. She took her time. She plumped out the coat and skirt with a currant bush that had ceased to earn its keep. She made a white cloth face, and with soot put features in. And she gave to the hat the forward tilt to which it had been accustomed.

Field Smith's humorous comment on the idea of female scarecrows in *Pearson's Magazine*, March 1933

She stood back at last. It was marvellous. The wind stirred the ample skirt till you would have sworn a woman moved there. She stared till her fixed eyes blurred the image. And then she was aware of a queer, sinking feeling in the pit of her stomach. It was *herself* standing there. She blinked, but still she stood. Both here and there she stood. It was very confusing.

Confusing it may have been to Mrs Cumming but, according to the writer, not only did the new scarecrow fool her neighbours – several of whom spoke to 'her' before realizing their mistake — but so familiar was the lady's own image to the birds that they assumed her stand-in was indeed her and gave it, and her crops, a wide berth. Could this substitution of a female for a male scarecrow herald a possible revolution in the gardens and corn-fields of Britain, Orgill MacKenzie asked in concluding his article.

Though there is no evidence of any such 'revolution' taking place, the idea certainly caught the imagination of one of the leading cartoonists of the day, Field Smith, who made his own wry comment in the form of the cartoon reproduced here of the embarrassed huntsman being thrown into the arms of a female scarecrow. It appeared in *Pearson's Magazine* in March 1933.

In the intervening years there are, though, reports from time to time of dressmakers' dummies being used as female scarecrows, and in January 1959 a Worcestershire farmer made headline news when he put up in one of his fields a life size, near-nude model of Brigitte Bardot which he had won in a cinema competition. Unfortunately, though, while the French 'sex-kitten' certainly kept away the birds, she attracted curiosity-seekers in droves, and the farmer was forced to remove the model in order to save his young crops from being trampled out of existence.

But if there was one person who gave an impetus to the idea of female scarecrows, it was almost certainly that setter of new trends the Princess of Wales, for certainly they became more in evidence around the countryside after a scarecrow made in her image (in company with the Prince) was featured in a national newspaper in July 1981. The story, which was headlined 'Royal Couple of Worzels' appeared in the *Sunday People*, complete with the photograph which is reproduced here.

> Fancy finding Charles and Lady Di standing there among the spuds [the paper commented]. The birds haven't had such a fright since Worzel Gummidge learned to talk. Which is exactly the result that the gardener Ray Gray hoped for.
>
> Ray's vegetable patch was being picked clean until he hit on the idea of appointing a couple of royal scarecrows. He pasted outsize pictures of Charles and Lady Diana on cardboard figures, draped some old clothes around them ... and waited to see what would happen.

THE TWENTIETH-CENTURY SCARECROW

The Lady Diana Scarecrow which started a new fashion in July 1981!

'They're working like a dream,' said 25-year-old Ray at home in Oak Hill, Havering, Essex, 'I think the birds are frightened to go anywhere near Charles with Lady Di around.'

'Which is just as it should be,' the paper added.
The immediate result of this story was a spate of female scarecrows, including a beautiful female dummy in a fashionable shirt and trousers which was spotted on an Essex smallholding by photographer Clive Penny, who promptly won a prize in the *Observer*'s weekly photographic competition. A Devonshire farmer, Bruce Burton, also put up a ten-foot-tall statue of the Venus de Milo on his land in June 1985. He had seen the status outside a bra factory that was in the process of being demolished and decided to save the half-ton figure from destruction. His wife, Sally, told a photographer from the *Mail on Sunday* newspaper who photographed the statue, 'I must admit I was jealous at first,

but we get on quite well ... and she makes an excellent scarecrow!'

Another farmer, George Moreton in Warwick, went a step further and put a whole bevy of former shop-window mannequins to work as scarecrows on his land. With over 500 acres to protect from crows and starlings, he bought the redundant models and – suitably clothed – arranged them across his fields. But so life-like did these lady scarecrows appear that he soon found himself with unexpected problems, as he explained in May 1986:

'First one of my neighbours thought someone had committed suicide on my land,' he said. 'They called the police when they saw a body lying beside an electric pylon. The neighbour was convinced the woman must have jumped to her death. In fact, it was just one of the models that the wind had blown over. Then there was the tragedy involving a combine harvester. The oil seed rape grew so quickly that the mannequin was completely covered up and when I came along the blades of the harvester just chewed her up.' None the less, he still swears by the efficiency of his remaining girl scarecrows.

Two teenaged Hampshire girls who went into the business of making scarecrows for local farmers also reported an increase in demand for female models. Kerry ten Kate and her friend Hilary Rattray said they made the figures from wood, hay and rags, finishing them off with neat little touches like suspender belts, petticoats and even handbags!

A spin-off from this latest development was the 'Scarecrow Look', a combination of casual wear and country clothes, which London gossip columnists reported as being the 'in thing' among certain groups of young people in the late autumn of 1986. However, the *Sunday Mirror*'s columnist Andrew Golden thought that, 'The scarecrow look is great down on the farm, but not really for the city's fashionable spots.'

Even the arrival of the female scarecrow has been unable to remove what some people now believe to be the greatest threat of all to the continued existence of the traditional scarecrow, for in the last few years modern technology has brought to bear on the age-old problem of protecting crops from birds – and some rather unusual mechanical 'scarecrows' have been the result.

Devonshire farmer Bruce Burton's statuesque Venus de Milo bird-scarer which he put up on his land in 1985

The first of these was 'Mr Fossygent' who appeared in October 1981 and was described as 'the scarecrow of the 1980s'. According to his inventors, two Suffolk men, John and Robert Foster, he no longer relies on wind power to function but is armed with microchips and powered by electricity.

'Fossygent' looks similar to a traditional scarecrow with an old hat and long coat but is actually a mechanical man with a 96 amp 12 volt battery for a heart which is activated by a photo-electric cell. As soon as dawn breaks, this triggers the figure into action turning his head and body and waving his arms. According to the two inventors, the secret of 'Mr Fossygent' is the frequency of his arm waving, which is synchronized to imitate the wing speeds of birds of prey like the kestrel. And in a flat field, fitted with a gas gun banger, it is said he can be effective over a 200-yard radius.

Another Suffolk engineer has come up with an idea based on the principle of using the image of a bird of prey to scare off smaller birds. In April 1983 Ronald Barrell of Heveningham unveiled an electronically controlled hawk which flies and swoops between two poles 200 feet apart, frightening everything in its path.

However, closer to the old idea of a scarecrow was 'Jon Doe' an inflatable figure invented in Ireland, made of tough PVC and mounted on a pole which was introduced to farmers in 1986. Ron Jackson, the man in charge of marketing 'Jon Doe' did have some words of comfort for the traditionalists when he said, 'We are confident that man, or imitation man, is still the most effective deterrent to birds.'

The most controversial of all the new inventions is, undoubtedly, the 'Space Age scarecrow', eight feet high, covered in irridescent paint, with three legs, a head in the form of an upturned tub, two frightening yellow eyes and long white arms fitted with streamers. It is the creation of Michael Williams of Saffron Walden in Essex, who says it '... wails like a ghost and sends out blinding flashes of light that are visible two miles away. He's the nearest thing to a real man running and shrieking across a field.'

The machine, or SS80 as it is prosaically called, is powered by a random-circuited motor which waves the arms and operates the air horns which make the terrifying sound. It

The bevy of beautiful scarecrows which caused unexpected problems for Warwickshire farmer, George Moreton, in 1986

also has the 'listening' device whereby other scarecrows or gas guns can trigger it into life at the same time.

Talking about his 'scarecrow', Michael Williams has explained, 'Scarecrows nowadays have a heavy duty job to perform, standing in a field day and night in all weathers through hurricane and snow. So they must be robust and corrosion-proof. We make ours of tough PVC fabric and steel and they can be sprayed in any colour.

'There is an electric motor inside the scarecrow which works off a car or tractor battery, and this can be set for as often and as long as the farmer requires. The thing comes to life with a loud screaming noise. Then there's a violent jerking movement with the head revolving at high speed that would probably scare Worzel Gummidge himself away!'

And with a not very flattering nod to the famous scarecrow, Michael Williams added, 'There's too much at risk today to leave it to dear old Worzel. Some vegetable crops are worth up to £200 a ton, and the huge acreages involved mean a harvest worth thousands.'

Certainly this new invention has already attracted enthusiastic orders from farmers in the USA, Japan and even Saudi Arabia, but it is a little premature to write off the traditional scarecrow just yet. He has rather too much history behind him to keel over and accept what journalist Jennifer Farley of the *Sunday Times* said of him after this latest invention came on the market: 'Worzel Gummidge move over,' she wrote, 'you may be about to join the already swollen ranks of the unemployed. It's a sad thought, but the harum-scarum scarecrow figure resplendent with straw-thatched head and broom-handle arms, may soon be as much a relic of the British farms as horse-drawn harvesters and pretty milkmaids.'

But not *so* fast! There are some farmers – and not a few members of the general public – who have a thing or two to say about this new breed of scarecrow.

To begin with, a spokesman of the National Farmers Union cautioned, 'There's no doubt that the most effective scarecrows rely upon noise as well as appearance. But many farmers still like the traditional scarecrow that resembles a man.'

And writing to the *Observer* in the wake of the launch of the 'Space Age scarecrow', Judith Gibson spoke for many others in a letter headed, 'Rural Calm Shattered':

> Electronic scarecrows, with their powerful air horns are, I am sure, of enormous value to farmers safeguarding their growing crops, but what of the people living within earshot who find their days – and often nights – punctuated by regular explosions? My husband and I have found our lives turned into misery when gas guns invaded our semi-rural area and night after night we found sleep impossible.
>
> The local environmental health officer was of tremendous help in persuading farmers to turn off the device at night. Much is written about noise, particularly from lorries and aircraft, but our move from the country to central London has given us peaceful and restful nights!

1986-7 has seen mounting support for such views. In October 1986 the council at Ryedale in North Yorkshire actually began offering local farmers £5 for every scarecrow

THE TWENTIETH-CENTURY SCARECROW

Scarecrows that SCARE – an amusing cartoon by Stan Fine (1982)

they erected on their lands. Explaining the reason for this, the council's tourist officer, Harold Mosley, said: 'A lot of visitors expect to see scarecrows in the countryside, but instead they find these noisy modern equivalents and they've taken a battering from new technology. We want to give a boost to tradition and prevent people instead of birds turning tail and heading for home!'

Then in Kent in March 1987, Suzy Gale, the wife of Roger Gale, the Conservative MP for Thanet North, announced the formation of BANG, 'The Bird Scarers Anti-Nuisance Group', aimed at combatting the noise of gas-cylinder bangers and electronic warblers. She explained to the press: 'When Roger and I moved to the country four years ago we hardly heard these contraptions, but there has been an incredible growth in their use. Last summer it was like living through the Battle of the Somme with endless salvoes day and night. I find it quieter in London!'

After Mrs Gale first wrote about this 'growing menace' to *The Times* newspaper in the summer of 1986, she received hundreds of letters – some from country dwellers who had moved house to escape the din. As a result she decided to form BANG, which will encourage its members to keep records of offending sounds and lobby their MPs. She says that, although farmers are urged by the NFU to use the noisy bird-scarers only during daylight – with a maximum of four bangs per hour, many ignore this.

If the creation of this group highlights a kind of crisis in the future of the scarecrow, a still more recent report offers some hope for it with the news that a number of farmers are said to be returning to certain old farming practices. Writing in *The Times* of 27 June 1987, David Nicholson-Lord declared under a headline 'Old Farming Practices Make a Comeback': 'A mixture of ancient farming practices and the latest scientific innovations could produce a new "green revolution". The value of the traditional methods is that they mimic natural ecological processes and make for sustained farming.'

This viewpoint was underlined by the *Sunday Telegraph*'s Agricultural Correspondent, David Brown, on 23 August 1987, when he wrote, 'While most farmers are using the latest technology and powerful combine-harvesters to keep them on target for another record-breaking cereal crop this year, a few still find a lucrative place for the old ways.'

If this *is* a new trend, clearly the scarecrow has, as ever, a part to play in the countryside.

Appendix:
How to make a Scarecrow

"*But, Arthur, should it be smi*"

Do-it-yourself scarecrow from *Punch*, 7 January 1976

Here are a few suggestions on the best way of making a scarecrow that *scares* – whether it is required for the wide-open acres of a farm or for the modest space of a smallholding or back garden.

Elizabeth Seager of *Amateur Gardening* focuses her attention on the small garden type of scarecrow:

> After Christmas, when berries and insects are scarce, birds will start to look for other tasty food, and they might decide to sample the cabbages and sprouts in your garden or allotment. A scarecrow can protect your crops and be fun to make.
>
> First make a wooden skeleton – just a strong six foot upright stake with a crossbar nailed across it at shoulder height, and a tin can nailed on for a head. Give this skeleton a padded body of plastic foam, straw or old rags tied around the stake with old nylon tights or twine. Paint a face on the tin head with waterproof paints and then dress your Worzel in old clothes.
>
> Most scarecrows I've seen lately have been wearing old jackets, trousers and caps, but long flapping hair under a straw hat and a fluttering skirt might scare the birds more.

Ever the humanitarian, Miss Seager add: 'Remember that if your Worzel is successful the birds will still be hungry, so provide food for them on a bird-table near the house where you can watch them feeding. Nuts, birdseed and kitchen scraps provided regularly with drinking water will help them survive the cold weather.'

Barbara Hargreaves of *Country Life* is an expert on the

field scarecrow and has some interesting observations to make on the different types:

> The ideal scarecrow should look as much like a human being as a few sticks and a bundle of old clothes can make him. If we don't set about constructing one with this object in mind we might as well save our time and energy. And this human being should be 'alive', doing something recognisably human. Standing up straight in the middle of a field with both arms stretched sideways is *not* a recognised human possibility. Try doing it yourself!
>
> But without departing from the use of sticks and old clothes I think we can still bring a scarecrow to life. We can, of course, make it look as if it is levelling a gun by adding a long, straight stick. Or we can put one of its arms in the air and make it look as if it is waving.
>
> A good test for a scarecrow of the latter type is to hide behind a hedge and wait for a passer-by to show up. When he does, shout a cheerful greeting still taking care not to be seen.

Care needs to be taken in choosing scarecrow names! (Cartoon by Martin Honeysett)

APPENDIX: HOW TO MAKE A SCARECROW

"People never send me anything useful. They send things like scarecrows which disclose a cocktail set"

A unique scarecrow by the ingenious W. Heath Robinson for Beverley Nichols' article 'Christmas and the Gardener', *Good Housekeeping*, December 1934

If he waves back at the scarecrow you've made a good job of it. If he asks it to come for a drink, emerge from your hiding place. To buy your silence he'll stand you more than one!

The artistic individual will not be content with a waving scarecrow, however, once he gets the knack of life-like arrangements. If, for instance, he used two bent pieces for the arms, dozens of fresh and fascinating combinations are made possible.

Some of these possibilities are, quite frankly, vulgar, and the farmer of taste will quickly, if a trifle wistfully, reject them. But others will suggest themselves, perhaps resulting in peering scarecrows – with one arm bent to the head and one to the hip, or even angry, fist-shaking scarecrows. Indeed, scarecrows, properly constructed, can serve the secondary purpose of expressing the personalities of their creators.

The happy farmer can make dancing scarecrows, kneeling scarecrows, stalking scarecrows. More, if we can equip a croucher with a couple of bottles, strapped together to represent binoculars, we shall have created what is surely the greatest bird-scarer of the lot – the Amateur Birdwatcher!

But like his fellow artists in the normal spheres of activity, the inspired scarecrow-constructor must fully exploit the potentialities of his simple materials without having to fall back on expensive trappings. He must do the best he can with old cast-off clothing and must never be tempted into using complete suits or fancy dress. Such Smart Alec practices should be left to his dilettante ex-theatrical neighbours!

Talking about neighbours, however, reminds me of one possible excuse for elaboration of dress. If the farmer does happen to have a neighbour he strongly dislikes, or a Ministry Inspector he particularly loathes, he may find deep satisfaction in dressing his scarecrows as near like these people as possible. Such visual insults, if well prepared and cunningly placed, can be far more telling than verbal!

Finally, an extra word of caution. Scarecrow-building can soon develop from a chore into a hobby, from a hobby into a real obsession.

After a life-time of interest in scarecrows and now a year in the writing of this book, I know what she means. The scarecrow does indeed have an enduring and irresistible charisma, that still has much to offer. You – and the birds – have been warned!

Select Bibliography

The distinctive symbol to be found on all the books from the American publishers, Scarecrow Press Inc.

The author's daughter, Gemma, with the Haining family scarecrows, Mawkin and Tatty-Bogle

Select Bibliography

During the course of writing I have consulted a great many books, but those which I found of the greatest interest and help in my research into the history and lore of scarecrows were the following:

Chambers, Robert, ed., *The Book of Days* (W. Chambers & Co., 1863)
Cobbett, William, *Rural Rides* (Peter Davies Ltd., 1930)
Copper, Bob, *A Song for Every Season* (Granada Publishing, 1975)
Haggard, Sir Henry Rider, *A Farmer's Year* (Cassell & Co., 1899)
Kitchen, Fred, *Life on the Land* (J.M. Dent & Sons, 1941)
Simpson, Jacqueline, *The Folklore of the Welsh Border* (Batsford, 1976)
Stephens, Henry, *The Book of the Farm* (William Blackwood & Sons, 1844)
Street, A.G., *Farmer's Glory* (Faber & Faber Ltd., 1932)
Thornbury, Walter, *Tour Around England* (Longmans Green, 1870)
Williamson, Henry, *Story of a Norfolk Farm* (Faber & Faber Ltd., 1941)
Wright, Joseph, *The English Dialect Dictionary* (Henry Frowde, 1903)

One of the pleasures in the writing of this book has been the discovery of quite a substantial number of varied and interesting short stories about scarecrows.

Anstey, F., 'Fawkes – Et Praeterea Nihil', *The Lost Load* (Longmans, 1904)
Brown, George Mackay, 'Master Scarecrow', *Fifth Ghost Book* (ed. Rosemary Timperley, Barrie & Jenkins, 1969)

Carr, W.H., 'Mrs Anstey's Scarecrow', *Ninth Pan Book of Horror Stories* (Pan, 1968)
Grahame, Kenneth, 'An Autumn Encounter', *Pagan Papers* (Bodley Head, 1898)
Hawthorne, Nathaniel, 'Feathertop', *Mosses from an Old Manse* (Frederick Warne & Co., 1846)
Jacobi, Carl, 'Witches in the Cornfield', *Weird Tales* (Arkham House, 1945)
Johnson, Roger, 'The Scarecrow', *The Year's Best Horror Stories* (ed. Karl Edward Wagner, Daw Books Inc., 1985)
Jones, Paul, 'Scarecrow', *Famous Short Stories* (ed. Frank C. Platt, New American Library, 1966)
Kneale, Nigel, 'Jeremy in the Wind', *Tomato Cain* (Collins, 1949)
de la Mare, Walter, 'The Scarecrow', *The Scarecrow & Other Stories* (Faber & Faber Ltd., 1945)
Martin, A.E., 'The Scarecrow Murders', *Ellery Queen's Mystery Magazine*, April 1948 (American Mercury Inc.)
Orczy, Baroness, 'The Old Scarecrow', *The Old Scarecrow & Other Stories* (Methuen, 1916)
Porges, Arthur, 'Josephus', *Fear!* May 1960 (Great American Publications)
Thurber, James, 'The Crow and the Scarecrow', *Further Fables for Our Time* (Hamish Hamilton, 1951)

Index

Index

Page numbers in italic indicate illustrations.

Addison, Joseph, 68-70
Africa, 158
Alldridge, Elizabeth, 92, 94
Apocalypse Now (film), 129
Arlen, Harold, 125
Arliss, George, 90, 117
Astor, Mary, 114
Atkinson, Frank, 139-40
Aunt Sally figure, 38
Australia, 158
Austria, 156

Balik, Fairuza, 129
BANG (Bird Scarers Anti-Nuisance Group), 171-2
Bardot, Brigitte, 164
Barrell, Ronald, 168
Basset, Fred, 24
Batchelor, Robin W., 15
Bates, Jonathan, 15
Baum, L. Frank, 78-82, 106-13
    books
        Dorothy and the Scarecrow of Oz, 109
        The Land of Oz, 109, 129
        Ozma of Oz, 129
        The Patchwork Girl of Oz, 110
        The Scarecrow of Oz, 111
        The Wonderful Wizard of Oz, 63, 64, 78-82, 106
    films
        His Majesty the Scarecrow of Oz, 111
        The Patchwork Girl of Oz, 110-11

    The Wizard of Oz, 109-10, 113-14, 119-28
Baum, L. Frank Jr., 111, 113
Berkshire, 23, 41
Besant, Sir Walter
    The World Went Very Well Then, 75
Berle, Milton, 131
Best, James, 54
Beaumont, Francis, and Fletcher, John
    Bonduca, 67
    The Wild-Goose Chase, 67
Bioscope, The, 103, 105
Blackmore, R.D.
    Christowell, 41
Blanc, Mel, 131
Bobbin, Paul
    Sequel, 59
Bolger, Ray, 12, 122-6
Bosworth, Hobart, 110
Bracknell, Berks., 23
Brown, David, 172
Brown, George Mackay
    'Mister Scarecrow', 101-2
Buchanan, William, 119
Burton, Bruce, 165, 167
Bury St Edmunds, Suffolk, 23-4

Campbelltown Courier, 154
Cameron, Sue, 116-17
Captain Clegg (film), 49, 118-19
Cara (magazine), 150
Carr, W.H.
    'Mrs Anstey's Scarecrow', 101
Carradine, John, 135, *136*, 137

cartoons and caricatures, 20, 21, 22, 23, 24, 25, 36, 39, 52, 148-9, 157, 159, 162, 163, 171, 176, 177
  see also film, animated
Case, Justin, 131
Cawley, Hon. Mrs Iris, 15
Chambers, Robert
  Book of Days, 38-40
Charles, Prince, *see* Wales, Prince and Princess of
Churchill, Charles, 71-2
clappers, 46
Clarens, Carlos, 115
Clephan Palmer, E., 48
Cobbett, William, 32-5, *36*
  Rural Rides, 32, *33*
  Weekly Political Register, 34
Cocks, Jay, 135
Collins, A.L., 146, *147*
Colwich, Shropshire, 21-3
Constanduros, Mabel, 138, *139*
Copper, Bob
  A Song for Every Season, 45-8
corn dollies, 60-1
corn spirits, 60-1
Couderc, Pierre, 110
Country Life, 21
Countryman, The, 101
Crocker, W.D., 152
Crop Chasers (film), 133
Cruikshank, George, *39*, *59*, *61*
Cushing, Peter, 118

Daily Mail, 19, 24, 26, 48-51, 52-3, 102, 137, 150
Daily Telegraph, 21
Daily Worker, 118
Dane, Clemence
  The Arrogant History of White Ben, 63, 86, 89-90
Daniels, Bebe, 110
Darante, William, 137
Dark Night of the Scarecrow (film), 137-8
dead birds, used as deterrent, 37-8, 48, 55-7, 70
de Felitta, Frank, 137
Defoe, Daniel
  Modern History of the Devil, 70-1
  Robinson Crusoe, 69, 70
de la Mare, Walter, 41, 63, 97-9
  'Crewe', 97
  'The Scarecrow or Hodmadod', 97-9
Denslow, W.W., *64*, 79, *79*, 124
Diana, Lady, *see* Wales, Prince and Princess of
Dickens, Charles
  Nicholas Nickleby, 72
Dorothy and the Scarecrow of Oz (Baum), 109
Dr Syn (film), 117
Dr Syn, Alias the Scarecrow (film), 104, 119, *120*
Dunning, Charles, 137
Dwan, Dorothy, 113

East Anglia, 23-4, 36-7, 42, 48-52, 150, 168-9
Ebsen, Buddy, 122-4
Elder, John, 118
Eliot, George, 75
  Adam Bede, 75
Ellery Queen's Mystery Magazine, 100
Emerson, David
  Son of the Fens, 42
English Countryman, The, 37
English Dialect Dictionary, 28

Famous Short Stories, 100
Farley, Jennifer, 170
Fear! (magazine), 159, *160*
Feigelson, J.D., 137
Ferguson, Otis, 119
fiction, scarecrows in
  as central character, 72-5, 76-8
  in children's stories, 78-84, 91-7
  earliest references, 63-8
  as sinister figure, 76-8, 84-6, 97, 100-2
  twentieth century, 78-102
Fielding, Andrew
  Scarecrow, 71
Fielding, Henry
  Joseph Andrews, 71

INDEX

film, scarecrows in, 26, *49*, 91, 103-6, 109-38
  Captain Clegg, *49*, 118-19
  Dark Night of the Scarecrow, 137-8
  Dr Syn, Alias the Scarecrow, 104, 119, *120*
  His Majesty, The Scarecrow of Oz (later *The New Wizard of Oz*), 111-13
  The Patchwork Girl of Oz, 110-11
  Puritan Passions, 75, 114-16
  The Rainbow Road to Oz, 129
  Return to Oz, 82, 129-31
  Scarecrow (short: Yugoslavia 1962), 133
  Scarecrow (US 1972), 135
  Scarecrow (short: UK 1972), 133-5
  The Scarecrow (France 1909), 103
  The Scarecrow (Denmark 1910), 104
  The Scarecrow (UK 1911), 104
  The Scarecrow (Italy 1912), 105-6
  The Scarecrow (France 1913), 106
  The Scarecrow (US 1920), 114
  The Scarecrow (short: E. Germany 1964), 133
  The Scarecrow (TV: US 1972), 116-17
  The Scarecrow (New Zealand 1982), 135-7
  The Wiz, 128
  The Wizard of Oz (1910), 110
  The Wizard of Oz (1925), *112*, 113-14
  The Wizard of Oz (1939), *12*, 119-28
film, animated, scarecrows in, 131-3
  Crop Chasers, 133
  Joe Scarecrow, 133
  Journey Back to Oz, 131, *132*
  Scarecrow (Hungary 1976), 133
  Scarecrow (Yugoslavia 1986), 133
  The Wizard of Oz (Japan 1984), 131
Fine, Stan, *171*
Fletcher, John *see* Beaumont, Francis
Fluck, Peter, 21
Folklore (magazine), 44
Foot, Michael, *20*, 21, 23
Foster, John and Robert, 168
Foster, Revd Stuart, 19
France, *155*, 156
Frazer, Sir James
  The Golden Bough, 60
Freedman, Lewis, 116
Fursdon, Dr Paul, 133

Gale, Suzy, 171-2
Gambon, Michael, 138
Garland, Judy, 122, *125*
Germany, 156
Gibson, Judith, 170
Gilkyson, Terry, 119
Gilliatt, Penelope, 118
Gillray, James, *36*
Glass, Murray, 111, 113
Glennon, Herbert, 110
Good Housekeeping, 177
Gottschalk, Louis, 110, 111
Grahame, Kenneth
  'An Autumn Encounter', 63, 76-8
Gray, Ray, 164-5
Guardian, 161
Gummidge, Worzel, *see* Worzel Gummidge

Hackman, Gene, 135
Haley, Jack, 122
Halloween, 159, *160*
Hall, Willis, 97, 140
Hamilton, Margaret, 131
Hamlin, Fred, 106
Hammer Films, 118
Harburg, E.Y. 'Yip', 125
Hardy, Oliver, 113, 114
Harper, Kenneth, 128
Harrington, Joy, 138
Hawkins, Irene, *98*
Hawthorne, Nathaniel
  'Feathertop', 63, 72-5, 114-17

Heath Robinson, W., *177*
Henfrey, Janet, 138
Hepworth, Cecil, 104, *105*
Hill, Maude, *116*
His Majesty the Scarecrow of Oz (film), 111
hodmadod, 28, 40-1
Hollywood Reporter, The, 116-17
Home Guard, 26
Honeysett, Martin, *176*
Horne, Lena, 128
Hungary, 157
Hunter, Glenn, 114
Hutchinson, Tom, 137
Hyett, Trevor, 135

Innes, Neil, 21
Ireland, *148-9*, 150-2
Italy, 156

Jack o'Kent, 44
jackolent, 28, 38-40, 57, 60-1, 66
Jackson, John
   Southward Ho, 59
Jackson, Michael, *127*, 128
Jackson, Ray, 17
Jackson, Ron, 168
Japan, 158, *159*
Jefferson, Thomas
   The Farm Book, 158
Joe Scarecrow (film), 133
Jones, Paul
   'Scarecrow', 100
Jonson, Ben
   The Staple of Newes, 68
   Tale of a Tub, 68
Journey Back to Oz (film), 131, *132*

Keaton, Buster, 114, *115*
Kent, 52-3, 171
King Hall, Edith
   The Story of the Scarecrow, 82-4
Kitchen, Fred
   Brother to the Ox, 41
Kossoff, David, 94, *95*
Kneale, Nigel, 41
   'Jeremy in the Wind', 101
Krenkel, Roy, *81*
Krokodil (magazine), *157*

Kummer, Frederic Arnold
   The Scarecrow Murders, 100-1

Lahr, Bert, 122
Land of Oz, The (Baum), 109
Larthe, Mrs Catherine, 14
Last Egyptian, The (film), 113
Laughlin, Anna, 108
Law, Roger, 21
Lawson, Nigel, 21
Lent, 38-9, 57, 60
Le Roy, Mervyn, 122
Lloyd, Robert, 71-2
Lockwood, Margaret, 117
Lofts, W.O.G., 58, 146
London Docks Authority Scheme, 21
London Standard, 131
Longleat House, *18*, 19
Lord's Cricket Ground, 26
Lower Slaughter, Glos., 146
Lumet, Sidney, 128

MacConnell, Cormac, 150-2
MacDonald, Murdo, 154
McGoohan, Patrick, *104*, 119, *120*
MacKaye, Percy
   The Scarecrow, 74-5, 114-17
MacKenzie, Orgill, 161-4
Maloney, Russel, 119
Mail on Sunday, 165
mammet/mommet, 28, 41
Marsh, Jean, 131
Martin, A.E.
   'The Scarecrow Murders', 100
Maskell, Henry P., 37, 57-8, 70, 146
mawkin, 28, 37, 38, 42, *43*, 58-9, 75
Mayer, Louis B., 122, 123
Menteth, Vera
   'The Scarecrow', 85-6
MGM, 119, 120, 122
Miller, Pip, *14*, 150
Minnelli, Liza, 131
Moffatt, Graham, 117
Montgomery, David, *107*, 108
Moore, Frank, 111
Morning Star, 135
Morrison, Ronald Hugh, 135
Moreton, George, 166, *169*

INDEX

Mosley, Harold, 171
Murch, Walter, 129
Murray, Charlie, 114
Museum of East Anglian Life, 23-4
Mussolini, Benito, 25, 26

National Farmers Union, 170, 172
Neil, John R., *130*, 131
New Music Express, 137
New Republic, The, 119
News of the World, 17
New Statesman, 102
New Yorker, The, 119
New York Times, 82, 161
New Zealand, 158
New Zealand Times, 101
Nicholson-Lord, David, 172
Nobody and Somebody, 30
Noyes, Alfred, 86, 87-8
   The Return of the Scarecrow, 87-9

Observer, 17, 118, 165, 170
'Old Jem' (Lord's scarecrow), 26
Oxford English Dictionary, 28, 38
Oxley, Shropshire, 146
Oz Film Manufacturing Company, 110-13
Oz stories, see Baum, L. Frank

Pacino, Al, 135
Palmer, Roy
   The Folklore of Warwickshire, 44-5
Passmore, John, 53
Patchwork Girl of Oz, The, 110
Pathé, Charles, 103
Pearson's Magazine, *163*, 164
Penny, Clive, 165
Perkins, Osgood, 114, 116
Pertwee, Jon, *16*, 19, 94, *96*, 138, 140-4
Pickard, James, 14
Pillsbury, Sam, 135
plastic, used on scarecrows, 16-17, 155-6, 168
Portugal, 156
Potter, Dennis, 138

Private Eye, 21
Pryor, Richard, 128
Puffin Books, 97, 102
Punch, 25, 26, 52
Puritan Passions (film), 75, 114-16

radio, 91-4, 116
Rainbow Road to Oz, The (film), 129
Raleigh, Sir Walter, 63, 65
   A Discourse on War, 65
Rattray, Hilary, 166
Raymond, John
   The Quiet Life, 41
Return to Oz (film), 82, 129-31
Rider Haggard, Sir Henry, 35, 36-7
   A Farmer's Year, 36-7
Rollings, Gordon, *118*, 119
Rooney, Mickey, 131
Ross, Diana, 128
Ross, Ted, 128
Rupert Bear, 21, *23*
Russell, Nipsey, 128
Ryedale District Council, 170-1

sacrifice, 55-7
Scarecrow, (short film; Yugoslavia 1962), 133
Scarecrow (film: US 1972), 135
Scarecrow (short film: UK 1972), 133-5
Scarecrow (animation: Hungary 1976), 133
Scarecrow (animation: Yugoslavia 1986), 133
Scarecrow, The (film: France 1909), 103
Scarecrow, The (film: Denmark 1910), 104
Scarecrow, The (film: UK 1911), 104
Scarecrow, The (film: Italy 1912), 105-6
Scarecrow, The (film: France 1913), 106
Scarecrow, The (film: US 1920), 114
Scarecrow, The (film: US 1982), 135-7

Scarecrow, The (play), 74-5, 114
  TV version, 116-17
'Scarecrow, The' (World War I code name), 24
Scarecrow Adventure (film), 133
'Scarecrow Look', 166
Scarecrow of Oz, The (Baum), 111
'Scarecrow Patrols' (World War II), 24
Scarecrow Press, 26, 27
Scarecrow of Romney Marsh, The (Dr Syn, Alias The Scarecrow), 119
scarecrows
  celebrities as, 23, 164-5
  contests, 21-4
  definitions, 28, 30
  female, 161-7, *169*
  in fiction, *see* fiction
  in film, *see* film
  human, 27, 30, 31, 32-4, 36, 44-54, 54-5
  as literary image, 31-2, 35
  magic associated with, 44
  mechanical, 166-72
  modern style, 16-17, 26, 155-6, 161, 168-72
  promotional use, 21, *143*, 144
  as sacrificial figure, 55-8, 60-1
  on television, *see* television
  in wartime, 24-6
Scarfe, Gerald, *20*, 21
Schatzberg, Jerry, 135
Schumacher, Joel, 128
Scotland, 42, 152-6
Scots Magazine, 155-6
Scotsman, The, 137
Sedge, Henry, 21-3
Selig Polyscope Company, 108-10
Semon, Larry, *112*, 113
Shakespeare, William, 38, 65-7
  Henry IV Pt 1, 65
  Henry VI Pt 1, 65
  Measure for Measure, 65, 66-7
  Merry Wives of Windsor, 38, 65, 66
Sharrad, John, 133-4
Shelley, Norman, 93
Shepard, E.H., 25

shoy hoys, 28, 32-4
Shropshire, 21-3, 35
Simpson, Dr Jacqueline, 59-60
Singing Detective, The, 138
Smalls, Charlie, 128
Smith, Field, *163*, 164
Smith, Monty, 137
songs, birdscarers', 45
Soutar, Willie, 154
Soviet Union, 158
Spain, 156
Spectator, The, 68-70
Spenser, Edmund
  The Faerie Queen, 63-5
SS Panzer Divisions, 26
Stagecoach (film), 110
Stephens, Henry,
  The Book of the Farm, 34-5
Stone, Fred, *107*, 108, 123
Stratford-on-Avon, 145-6
Street, A.G.
  Country Calendar, 40-1
  Ditchampton Farm, 40
Stubbs, Una, 142
Sunday Express, 17-19
Sunday Mirror, 166
Sunday People, 164
Sunday Telegraph, 172
Sunday Times, 21, 170
Sussex, 45-8
Sutherland, Hal, 131
Syn, Dr, 90-1, 117-19

tattie-bogle/bogie, 28, 42, 152-6
tattie-doolie, 42
television
  The Scarecrow, (US), 116-17
  The Scarecrow of Romney Marsh (US), 119
  The Singing Detective (UK), 138
  Worzel Gummidge (UK), 138-44
Ten Commandments, The (film), 110
Thatcher, Margaret, 23
That's Dancing (film), 126
Thomas, Danny, 131
Thornbury, Walter
  A Tour Round England, 35

INDEX

Thorndyke, Russell, *90*, 90-1, 117-19
Thurber, James
   'The Crow and the Scarecrow', 99-100
Thynne, Christopher, *18*, 19
Tietjens, Paul, 106
Time, 119, 135
Times, The, 19, 172
   correspondence columns, 13-17, 172
Timpson, John, 150
Todd, Barbara Euphan, 63, 91-7, 138
   Worzel Gummidge, *92*, 94-7
Treasury, The, 57-8, 70
Treddlehoyle, Tom
   Bairnsla Ann, 59
Turner, Otis, 109
Turner, Phil, 53-4
Tuttle, Frank, 114-15

United States, 158-61

Venus de Milo, 165, *167*
video cameras, used in scarecrows, 161, *162*

Wade, Philip, 93
Wales, Prince and Princess of, 164-5
Walker, Alexander, 131
Walpole, Sir Hugh
   The Golden Scarecrow, 86-7
Walt Disney Organization, 119, 120
Waltham, Eddie, 52-3
wartime, scarecrows in, 24-6
Waterhouse, Keith, 97, 142
Warwickshire, 41, 44-5, 145-6, 166
Westall, Robert
   The Scarecrows, 102
Westminster Review, 75
Wherry, B.A., 44
White, Garry Michael, 135
Wilder, Gene, 116-17
Willers, Terry, *148-9*
Williams, Michael, 168-9
Williamson, Henry
   The Story of a Norfolk Farm, 42-4
Williamson, Nicol, 131
Wilson, Thomas
   The Art of Rhetorique, *29*, 30-2
Wiltshire, 40
Wiz, The (film), 128
Wizard of Oz, The
   animated film (1982), 131
   film (1910), 110
   film (1925), *112*, 113-14
   film (1935), *12*, 119-28
   musical play, 106-8
Wonderful Wizard of Oz, The (Baum), 12, 63, *64*, 78-82, 106
World War I, 24
World War II, 24-6
Wormser, Gwendolyn Ranger
   'The Scarecrow', 84-5
Worzel Gummidge stories, *16*, 19-21, 86, 91-7
Wright, Hugh, E., 93
Wright, Joseph, 28

Yorkshire, 41, 170-1

SPRING GREEN COMMUNITY LIBRARY
230 E. Monroe Street
Spring Green, WI 53588